"Direct, actionable, and true, this is an urgent call to embrace learning. The world is changing faster than ever, and a good book can be your shortcut to the change you seek to make."

Seth Godin, author of *The Practice*

"Victor Hugo once said, '*To learn to read is to light a fire.*' How true this is! Brown and Wisnewski perfectly capture the essence of reading power in their terrific book *Read to Lead*. This book is filled with excellent tips, advice, and suggestions on both why and how to expand your horizons through reading and how to make it a daily habit that will serve you for a lifetime. The readers of today are truly the leaders of tomorrow. A splendid, worthwhile read!"

Stephen M. R. Covey, *New York Times* and #1 *Wall Street Journal* bestselling author of *The Speed of Trust*

"If you have the nagging feeling that you should read more but can't seem to do it, this book is for you. *Read to Lead* provides research-backed motivation to become a reader. And it gives you the practical tips and techniques you need to get the most out of every book you choose—which in turn makes reading extremely valuable and enjoyable. Let Jeff and Jesse guide you in your new reading routine."

Michael Hyatt, *New York Times* bestselling author and founder of LeaderBooks

"I might be biased because I'm a writer, but I think books are the cheapest, easiest way to radically change your life. In this book, Jeff and Jesse take that idea and supercharge it with actionable steps you can begin using to improve your career instantly."

Jon Acuff, *New York Times* bestselling author of *Soundtracks: The Surprising Solution to Overthinking*

"Reading is the freedom that leads to all other freedoms. *Read to Lead* will inspire accelerating readership, growth, and entrepreneurship. I hope it excites everyone who can read (4 billion of us) to teach one who can't to read (4 billion alive now). I am happy you are reading and leading with my friends' book."

Mark Victor Hansen, bestselling author and cocreator of the Chicken Soup for the Soul, One Minute Millionaire, and ASK! series

"If you want to read more and retain more, Jeff and Jesse have amassed a treasure trove of practical ideas for you. In Read to Lead you will find hundreds of best practices you can use to revolutionize the way you read."

Mark Miller, vice president of High Performance Leadership, Chick-fil-A, Inc., and international bestselling author of *Win Every Day*

"This extraordinary book will change your life, unlock your potential, and enable you to achieve any goal you can set for yourself. The richest and most successful people in the world have read themselves to riches and great rewards, often starting with little or nothing, and so can you."

Brian Tracy, speaker, author, consultant, and self-made millionaire

"Jeff and Jesse have written a must-read book about the life-changing act of reading. They start *Read to Lead* by sharing inspiration and science-backed motivation to read more. Then they lay out easy-to-adopt ideas that will help you read faster—and fully absorb what you read. Finally, they share creative ways to bring books to life and take your newfound knowledge from page to people. Whether you're an avid reader or an aspiring one, *Read to Lead* will arm you with ideas and inspiration that allow the wisdom trapped in books to guide your path through life."

Pamela Wilson, author of *Master Content* books

"Growing up in a poor farming family with no radio or TV, I found books to be my lifeline to a broader world. Those books took me to places around the world, allowed me to learn from the brightest minds in history, and opened the doors to a life of richness and joy. Books are my most prized possessions today, not because of their monetary value, but because of what they represent in transforming my life. Here's a guide to enhance your life and explode your opportunities for leading well."

Dan Miller, author of *48 Days to the Work You Love* and host of the *48 Days Podcast*

READ TO LEAD

READ

— TO —

LEAD

THE SIMPLE HABIT THAT EXPANDS YOUR
INFLUENCE AND BOOSTS YOUR CAREER

JEFF BROWN AND JESSE WISNEWSKI

BakerBooks

a division of Baker Publishing Group
Grand Rapids, Michigan

© 2021 by Jeffery D. Brown and Jesse Wisnewski

Published by Baker Books
a division of Baker Publishing Group
PO Box 6287, Grand Rapids, MI 49516-6287
www.bakerbooks.com

Library of Congress Cataloging-in-Publication Data
Names: Brown, Jeffery D., 1966– author. | Wisnewski, Jesse, 1980– author.
Title: Read to lead : the simple habit that expands your influence and boosts your career / Jeffery D. Brown and Jesse Wisnewski.
Description: Grand Rapids, MI : Baker Books, [2021] | Includes bibliographical references.
Identifiers: LCCN 2021009308 | ISBN 9781540901200 (paperback) | ISBN 9781540901736 (casebound) | ISBN 9781493430253 (ebook)
Subjects: LCSH: Reading.
Classification: LCC PN83 .B783 2021 | DDC 418/.4—dc23
LC record available at https://lccn.loc.gov/2021009308

Published in association with the literary agency of Legacy, LLC.

21 22 23 24 25 26 27   7 6 5 4 3 2 1

DEDICATION FROM JEFF

To Matt "Austin" Shuff and Seth Godin who, though they've never met, teamed up with one another in 2003 to help reignite my love for reading.

To my mother, Peggy, and my late father, Joseph, for an incredibly loving childhood.

And to everyone who has ever listened to the *Read to Lead* Podcast. Without your support the last eight years, this book would simply not exist.

DEDICATION FROM JESSE

To Jessica, my beloved, you fill my life with love (and the words to write).

To my children, Peyton, Jude, Elizabeth, Jonah, and Evelyn, I pray you pick up and carry on a love for reading.

CONTENTS

INTRODUCTION

WHY READ A BOOK ABOUT READING BOOKS

Today a reader, tomorrow a leader.

Margaret Fuller

Considering you're reading a book about reading books for professional development, it's likely you already value both of those things. Regardless of whether you're a non-reader, sporadic reader, or bibliophile, or you are early in your career or are a C-level executive, reading this book tells us you're interested in improving your reading, sharpening yourself professionally, or progressing in your career or business. It also lets us know you either feel stuck or you're looking for some tips in taking your reading, influence, and profession to the next level. But you don't know what to do next. You have questions:

- Will books help me to improve myself?
- What books should I read?
- How can I apply what I read?
- Is there a way I can remember more of what I read?

- How can I read faster?
- Is listening to audiobooks or reading book summaries enough?

Thankfully, you're in the right place. Books can transform you as a person and professional. And the act of reading itself possesses the ability to improve your decision-making skills, increase your intelligence, and open up more opportunities, among several other benefits. To milk the books you read for all they're worth, all you need to do is capture a vision for reading and learn a handful of lessons on choosing what to read and how to read. Afterward, you'll be well on your way to creating an unchangeable reading habit that will fuel your career and business. In this book, we're going to show you how.

Before getting into the details, let's get a few things out of the way.

What Does It Mean to Read to Lead?

As President Harry S. Truman said, "Not all readers are leaders, but all leaders are readers."[1]

There's way more to reading to lead than strictly reading leadership books, though they certainly can be on your reading list. Reading to lead is more about how reading itself can make you a better son or daughter, friend, coworker, manager, entrepreneur, and an overall better human being. As you read books in general, you'll better understand people, improve your decision-making skills, sharpen your ability to communicate, and become more creative, which are all essential characteristics of the modern-day leader.

Does this mean I should only read whatever book I fancy at the moment?

Nope.

Far from it.

What you'll see in the following chapters are the benefits associated with reading all sorts of books—including fiction and books you find entertaining. What you'll also discover are ways you can identify nonfiction books you should read to learn skills, and how to (nearly) master anything through the books you read, along with a few tips on how to reinforce these lessons.

So reading to lead includes a combination of the act of reading and what you read. As you read—and read books related to skills, disciplines, and characteristics relevant to your work—you'll be better positioned than others to "take the lead" in life and business.

Special Skills Are Not Required

Reading books requires one skill: reading.

For millions of adults in the United States, this is a challenge. There's no need to feel ashamed if this is you, nor is there any reason to judge someone else who has this problem. Later, we'll cover reasons why someone may be a nonreader. And if this is you or someone you know, there's help available.

Assuming you're able to read, you don't need to acquire additional skills to reap the benefits from books. You don't need to take out a ginormous student loan. You don't need to obtain a high-priced certificate. And you don't have to stop working or going to school to read more books. At times, this may be what's best for you for different reasons. But don't shy away from reading books and enjoying the benefits they provide.

In your career and business, often you can make tremendous strides or discover new opportunities from reading books. As you'll see later, there's really no comparison between the cost of books and the return on investment (ROI) they provide compared to an expensive degree, graduate school, or certificate.

Start Reading Anytime

Haven't read a book in months, years, or decades?

No sweat. You can start reading more today.

Jeff didn't pick up a book for a twelve-year period spanning his twenties and thirties. For Jesse, on the other hand, the first book he read on purpose was when he was twenty years old. We're not alone. Countless others have discovered later in life the joy and benefits of reading books.

As you ramp up your reading regimen, don't copy the reading habits of someone else or feel like a failure if you're not reading dozens of books or more a year. Focus on creating a reading plan that suits your needs and fits with your season of life—later, we'll show you how.

> **Fight away regret.**
> **Don't compare yourself to others.**
> **Start reading more—today.**
> **Your future self will thank you later.**

Reading Lessons and Tips in One Place

Between Jeff and me (Jesse), it has taken years of reading, a couple of courses, research, and interviews with hundreds of authors to come away with the lessons contained within these pages. We're not tooting our own horn. Instead, we want you to know you can reduce your learning curve, maximize your reading, save yourself time and money in learning, and position yourself to progress professionally with the lessons in this book.

We'd love nothing more than for you to take these lessons, apply them in your life, and succeed at whatever work you do.

How to Read This Book

Here are three ways you can get everything out of *Read to Lead*.

1. Pick and Choose What You Read

We wrote *Read to Lead* in such a way that you can choose whatever chapter you want to read. Ideally, it's best to read the first part ("Why You Need to Read Books") in order to capture a vision for reading. But the chapters can be read individually. If you must, or if you're pressed for time, feel free to look at the table of contents to see what resonates with you and get to work.

2. Use This Book as a Reference

Several of the chapters contain lessons you'll need to practice and helpful tips you'll need to use before reading your next book. We recommend spending as much time as you need when it comes to building a reading plan, creating a reading habit, and increasing your reading speed. It will also be helpful to refer to chapter 8, "How to Absorb a Book into Your Bloodstream," before you read a new book to prepare yourself to comprehend and retain what you read.

3. Download These Resources

Throughout this book, you'll see multiple resources mentioned that you can download for free. You can wait to download these resources later. Or you can go ahead and visit readtoleadbook.com/resources to see what's available and access them now.

That's all for now.

Let's get started.

PART 1

WHY YOU NEED TO READ BOOKS

CHAPTER 1

Why You Need to Read Like Your Career Depends on It

*Reading is essential for those who seek
to rise above the ordinary.*

Jim Rohn

Man, not again.

The thought raced through my (Jesse's) head.

The writing was on the wall.

I was working for a nonprofit organization as a copywriter, and the organization was going through internal changes. I had a hunch my job would be phased out.

Not knowing if I was going to have a job twisted my stomach into an awful knot. My family and I had just moved to Washington state from West Virginia so I could take this position, and now the security of my job was fading away. It's hard to live life, do good work, and provide for your family when your job security is in question.

For a while, I just hoped for the best. I continued to perform my duties faithfully, and like a wannabe professional poker player, I hid my stress, kept my cool, and held my cards close to my chest. But the fear of not knowing was too much for me to bear for long. So, instead of waiting to be acted upon, I decided to take action.

Since I wanted to stay with the organization, I started to look for ways I could make an internal pivot. I was on a quest to discover a different job within the organization. Thankfully, I had an idea of what that might be.

When I first accepted my position as a copywriter, I was new to the field. I had a breadth of writing experience—mostly in academic papers, trade books, and blog posts—but I wasn't adept as an ad man. To get myself up to speed, I read several copywriting books. I digested the classics, like *The Adweek Copywriting Handbook*, *Ogilvy on Advertising*, and *The Copywriter's Handbook*. I also explored several current titles. Reading these books exposed me to new ways of sharing messages, reaching people, and building a brand. While I enjoyed the art of writing, through reading I developed an interest in the science of managing and marketing a message. Coincidentally, I learned there was a potential role for such a job within my organization—a job in content strategy.

However, I wasn't ready to make a transition. I knew I needed further training to prepare myself, but I ran into two significant problems: time and money.

At this period of my life, I was still in graduate school pursuing a religious degree. I didn't have the ability to pursue additional coursework. I couldn't give up my current studies, and I wasn't sure how long my job would last. What is more, being married with four kids (at the time) and working for a nonprofit organization didn't leave me with any time or money to spare to take classes or online courses. After ruling out a few ideas, there was one last thing I knew to do: hit the books!

Before I approached my organization about my interest in learning more about content strategy, I learned everything I could about the topic within a few short months. The year was 2013, so there wasn't a ton on the market. But I did find several helpful books, such as

Content Strategy for the Web by Kristina Halvorson and Melissa Rach

Content Strategy for Mobile by Karen McGrane

Clout by Colleen Jones

The Web Content Strategist's Bible by Richard Sheffield

Content Rules by Ann Handley and C. C. Chapman

The New Rules of Marketing and PR by David Meerman Scott

Managing Content Marketing by Joe Pulizzi and Robert Rose

Hungry to learn a new skill, I devoured these books. I chewed on every last word, digested new concepts, and took what I learned to build a proposal. By spending a little more than $100 on books and many hours absorbing their content, I gained the confidence and skills I needed to make a move.

I shared my idea with my supervisor, who liked it; the transition went smoothly, and I was able to pursue different work within the organization. Were it not for the knowledge I gained from the books I read, I would not have been able to make such a pivot. Through no fault of my own or ill will from the organization, I would have been left out in the cold. Crazy enough, this wasn't the only time I've had to make such a transition. I've made several professional changes, and I've had to learn new skills along the way.

Now, I'm not a multimillionaire, nor will my life experiences and exploits fill the pages of history books. I have not accomplished great feats that have been recognized by the world, the United States of America, my hometown, or even my wife. But I have landed jobs with internationally recognized organizations—jobs I had no business landing on paper. And I did it through something as simple and life changing as reading.

The Times, They Are a-Changin'

Over the past ten years, I've gone through several professional transitions. Here's a snapshot of my seemingly sporadic work experience:

insurance sales (personal and business)
retail store manager
pastoral ministry
call center sales representative
copywriting
content management
marketing manager
director of marketing

For many years, I wrestled with the changes I've gone through. When I was in high school, I assumed I would go to college and then work, raise a family, and retire. I had this idea that my life would follow a straight line from beginning to end. It turns out my professional career has looked more like an EKG of a cardiac patient. It's up and down and all over the place.

On the one hand, some of my transitions were on purpose. For example, I initially obtained a bachelor's degree in marketing, pursued a career in insurance, and then decided to resign from that line of work to become a pastor. To make this change, I had to make a hard turn professionally.

After I resigned from my insurance career, I moved to a different state and participated in an unofficial internship with a local church. This wasn't an easy part of life. From working in a fabric and craft store, to managing an ice cream shop, to waiting tables on nights and weekends, I did whatever I had to do to make ends meet.

The apartment I stayed in had faded red shag carpet on the wall and golden-laced velvet wallpaper in one of the bathrooms. To this day, I don't know whether or not I should have vacuumed the walls.

On the other hand, some of my professional transitions were somewhat out of my control. I left one job and a field I loved to pursue a new adventure before the organization imploded for a variety of reasons. For another job, I did something stupid (well, unwise) and chose to resign from my position because I had stirred up the proverbial hornet's nest. There was a different job I took between transitions that wasn't a good fit at all. It was like I was a square peg being crammed into a round hole, which meant things didn't work out for long. I'm not sure if you've ever found yourself in one of these situations, but it's never a party finding a new job when your back is against the wall.

Enter Jeff Brown

I (Jeff) had a similar experience—working at several different jobs instead of maintaining one simple career path. For a brief period in my early twenties, a wonderful coworker took me under his wing and gave me books from Zig Ziglar and Og Mandino to read.

I was working on the air at a local radio station and toying with the idea of becoming a radio ad salesman like him (that's where the "real money" was at, I was told). These books, he thought, would help me get started. I enjoyed them well enough, but I struggled a great deal with how to *apply* what I was reading. That, I soon realized, was a separate skill all its own. It didn't help that I wasn't convinced I even wanted to be in sales, real money or not (turns out I didn't).

It would be about twelve years before I picked up another book. During that span, I would hold no fewer than eight jobs in three cities. My longest tenure at any one of them was just twenty-two months, and I was fired from five of them.

Partway through, for about four years, I changed careers, leaving radio to work in the music business before coming back to radio. In that four-year span, I worked for four record labels:

label 1—twenty-two months
label 2—twelve months
label 3—twelve months
label 4—five weeks

That last stint was actually the one record label I *didn't* get fired from. Yes, your math is correct. After three weeks on the job, I put in my two week's notice.

I'm not proud of that (and my boss sure was miffed), but leaving that position for my next job turned out to be one of the best decisions I've ever made.

I would begin that job in May 2000 but, unlike all the others up to this point, I not only managed to hang on to it for longer than a few months but would go on to be promoted a total of six times in a span of thirteen years. And to what do I attribute this turn of events? How did I go from

KRISTY CONE, ASSISTANT REGIONAL DIRECTOR, FDIC, ON THE READING LIFE:

In my mid-twenties, reading became a key component of my strategy of becoming better. My career has been in the banking industry, and I read mostly nonfiction in topics of business, economics, personal finance, biographies, history, leadership, and personal growth. But over the years, I have also explored other situational topics depending on my season of life, such as religion and spirituality, grief and loss, relationships, trauma, psychology, and human behavior. I cannot imagine what I would be like without the counsel and instruction from books—I am a functioning adult because of what I've read in books, from personal study, group discussions, and one-on-one interactions, both giving and receiving counsel and advice. It's to a point where in any given conversation, my mind is thumbing through my mental index of books and concepts, and my responses are a composite of decades of learning from others via reading. In the past year, I got a significant promotion at work, the culmination of applying decades of study and learning to prepare me for this role. It's the "fourth quarter" of my career, and reading books has given me tools, insights, and confidence to "finish well."

job-hopping maniac to valued employee, one with a disdain for the status quo? Quite simply, I became serious about my own professional growth. More specifically, in 2003 I began a habit of intentional and consistent reading. This habit would also turn out to be largely responsible for instilling in me the confidence to venture out on my own when this last season came to an end in 2013.

Your professional career might look similar to our experience. You may go to college to do one thing, and then figure out that you want to do something else. You may get fired from your job for whatever reason. Or you might feel stuck in your current gig without the hope of moving up or moving on. Whatever your career path, you're sure to hit a bump or two along the way.

We don't mean to be the bearers of bad news, but gone are the days when you could go to college, work for the same employer, and live in the same town until you retire.

We understand this may be the case for some professions—such as nurses, doctors, lawyers, accountants, and teachers—who tend to have a more linear professional development. But most people experience significant career changes. Here are some sobering statistics.

- The average employee tenure is 4.6 years.[1]
- The average millennial tenure is less than three years.[2]
- The life expectancy of a company on the S&P 500 is barely fifteen years.[3]

Add to this the growing trend in the United States workforce toward hiring contingent workers (e.g., contract, part-time), and you can see that job security is a vapor.[4] Here today. Gone tomorrow.

You may go through ten or fifteen different jobs during your career. If you're a millennial, this number will most likely be higher. Recent studies discovered that millennials will change jobs at least four times before they're thirty-two.[5]

Our aim in telling you this isn't to dash your dreams against the rocks. Think of it more like us waving smelling salts under your nose to wake you up to the reality most of us will face.

It's time to step up and get ready for these new challenges!

But where do we start? How can we prepare ourselves for this new economic reality?

Simple.

We set a new target.

The Economic Imperative of Becoming a Lifelong Learner

For years, the age-old wisdom in the United States has been this:

- Get a college degree.
- Get a job.
- Start a family.
- Retire.

Well, this advice has some merit to it. But today, it's incomplete.

At one point in US history, obtaining a college degree would place you in a position to get a job and stay employed with the same company for years. It was important what school you went to and what course of study you pursued. But today, getting a bachelor's degree is merely a prerequisite for many jobs, and you aren't guaranteed to get a job in your field of study. Research has found that two-thirds of college graduates have a job that requires a bachelor's degree, but only 27.3 percent of these graduates are in a job directly related to their field of study.[6] For example, if you're studying literature, you might find yourself working in advertising.

Yeah, probably not what you expected.

Getting a college degree is an important first step, but it's not the end. To prepare yourself for the new economic challenges you will face, you need to set your sights on becoming a lifelong learner.

This isn't something you can be passive about. According to a recent report by *The Economist*, lifelong learning is becoming an economic imperative.[7] In other words, we need to be constantly learning. We have to have our eyes on obtaining new skills and gaining different experiences to ensure our professional marketability.

A lifelong learner is someone who is self-motivated and committed to gaining new knowledge and skills. You have many ways to accomplish this goal—you can get a new degree, obtain a graduate certificate, or take online courses. At times, some of these options may be best for you and what you want to accomplish. But one of the best, most affordable, and flexible ways you can improve yourself professionally is by reading books.

Reading books may not appear on your résumé or Linked In profile. But the benefits you reap from what you read will. Reading books will help you learn new skills, improve your decision-making abilities, and even provide you with more professional opportunities. Reading books can also help you avoid costly mistakes and reduce your learning curve.

If you need help solving a problem, overcoming an obstacle, or getting unstuck, then look for a book on whatever you're going through. Unless you're a glutton for pain and punishment, there's no need to reinvent the wheel if someone else has already gone through what you're going through now. In the words of comedian Groucho Marx, "Learn from the mistakes of others. You can never live long enough to make them all yourself."[8]

Think about it like this: on your job or in your business, you will have endless opportunities to learn new things. From mastering new skills to growing in your ability to lead others, every week you will have a chance to grow. Now, will you haphazardly approach these moments with little preparation and reflection? Or will you embrace them by doing what you can and reading whatever book may help you improve yourself? Well, what if we said reading books will boost your performance and help you to work better with others? Would you devote yourself to reading more books? We hope so.

If you want to build a successful career or business, then we encourage you to read—a lot. Reading is a common habit shared by most successful people throughout history. From Bill Gates, Florence Nightingale, Booker T. Washington, and Warren Buffett to Abraham Lincoln, Margaret Thatcher, Theodore Roosevelt, and Winston Churchill, many successful people devoted significant amounts of their time to reading books.

The benefits of reading are many. Yet today, people are reading less than before. This growing decline in reading creates an opportunity for you to learn new skills, rise above your competition, and build a successful career by reading books.

Over to You

Today is the best day to embrace lifelong learning. Yesterday is gone. Tomorrow isn't guaranteed. Today—the moment you are reading these words—is the time to pause, reflect, and assess how well you are doing. In other words, it's time to know how many books you've read, are reading, and have left to read during your lifetime.

We understand self-assessments can be difficult, and it's never pleasant to talk about the end of your life. But taking the time to calculate how many books you have left to read has a way of focusing your attention. At least this is what Max Joseph discovered.

To overcome his bookstore anxiety and read more books, Max Joseph, a filmmaker and television host, shot a short film documenting his quest.[9] For his film, he spoke with a variety of people to help him tackle his TBR (to be read) list.

One of his interviewees, Tim Urban, shared an insightful lesson that will strike FOMO (fear of missing out) in the heart of anyone who has ever thought about reading more books. In his interview, Tim asked Max how long he might live (barring any unforeseen events), how old he was that day, and how many books he read per year to estimate how many books he would read in his lifetime. When doing the math, Tim allowed Max to feel the weight of his current reading habits so he could see that if he didn't make a change, he would only read fifty-five more books during the rest of his life. Needless to say, Max wasn't thrilled with the answer to this math equation.

This is a helpful exercise, and one we encourage you to do—right now. Take two or three minutes to fill in this equation for yourself:

How many books will you read during the rest of your life? Do you feel like gloating about your results? Or does it stress you out? For most people, including ourselves, this math equation is enough to light a fire underneath anyone who has a fleeting interest in reading more books.

In the following pages, we will share lessons with you to clarify what you need to read, how to read (a lot of) books, and different strategies you can use to retain and apply what you read. Hopefully, by the end of this book, you'll come back to this equation and feel better about your results.

Further Reading

These books will lead you into further exploring your professional development:

Linchpin: Are You Indispensable? by Seth Godin

How to Win Friends and Influence People by Dale Carnegie

The Call: Finding and Fulfilling God's Purpose for Your Life by Os Guinness

Extreme Ownership: How U.S. Navy SEALs Lead and Win by Jocko Willink and Leif Babin

CHAPTER 2

Eight Research-Backed Reasons Why Readers Do Better in Their Careers

You will be the same person in five years as you are today except for the people you meet and the books you read.

Charlie "Tremendous" Jones

The books you read can transform you. Like a chemical reaction, in which you add one or more substances together to create one or more different substances, each book you read is like introducing a new substance into your life that will create something new. From what you believe and the skills you learn to reducing your stress and creating more professional opportunities, reading books will make a life-changing difference.

This was the case for me (Jeff).

I jumped at the chance to reenter radio. Four years in the music business was enough for me. In my new radio job, it wasn't long before I realized how fortunate I was to have been given this chance. The station had a stellar reputation in the industry nationwide. The line of people who would have loved to work at the company was a mile long, and positions like the one I was to fill didn't open up very often. I was to take over the afternoon show from the man who would be my boss, Matt, allowing him to go off the air completely and focus on his managerial duties (Denise, his wife, joked that I was her favorite employee, as I helped bring her husband home in time for dinner again).

I shudder to think where I would be in my life and career today if not for Matt and his decision to hire me. Matt is, without a doubt, the best leader I've ever had the chance to work with. The things he taught me and the values he instilled in me can never be repaid. One of those values was reading.

I remember discovering, not long after I began working there, that members of the leadership team would gather once a week in the conference room and discuss a book they were all reading. I would be at my desk or in the studio during these meetings, wondering what their conversations sounded like. What were they discussing? What were they learning? What epiphanies were taking place? What eureka moments might I be missing? Why did I care? Why now?

Simply put, this group of people was different. In just a short time I came to admire them and the "product" they'd built. The wider industry admired the company's leadership as well. The culture was one that welcomed ideas from all sides. Standards were high, and learning was ongoing.

Much of that learning came from books. This was not something I'd ever heard or seen before. To my knowledge, none of the staff at the companies I'd worked for up to this point (remember, it was a lot of companies) were reading books as a means to hone their craft.

I was fascinated by the idea that a bunch of radio people from all different backgrounds were intentionally reading business books with the goal of being better employees, better talent, and better humans. And it gradually became clear to me that one of the reasons, if not the main reason, this group of employees led the industry was because they were unwilling to settle. They never assumed they knew—or would ever know—everything. They avoided the status quo at all costs. They understood the value of inviting in outside mentors, and that one of the easiest and most effective ways to do that was through the right books.

This experience helped to get me thinking long term about my career for really the first time. To borrow a phrase my mom was fond of using in my youth, I was beginning to distinguish my "tail from a hole in the ground."

All I knew was I wanted to be in that room. Eventually, I was invited in. I'm not sure what prompted it, but maybe they had grown tired of my ongoing questions about the books being read and the concepts being learned. Hey, "squeaky wheel." Am I right?

My entry into this coveted group could not have been timed any better. Early on, I was exposed to books like *Good to Great* by Jim Collins, *The Five Dysfunctions of a Team* by Pat Lencioni, and *Purple Cow* by Seth Godin, which completely altered the trajectory of my life and career.

Reading books can actually change you—for the better. According to a wealth of research and studies, reading books can increase your professional opportunities, enhance your decision-making skills, and make you a better overall leader.

Yet, today, as we'll point out in chapter 3, people are reading less than before.

Even though this decline in reading is troubling on many levels, it does provide you with a great opportunity to get ahead. "A readership crisis is really a leadership crisis," wrote Michael Hyatt. "And for people who know how to respond, *crisis* is just another way of saying *opportunity*."[1]

As a reader, you can rise above your competition, grow yourself as a leader, and obtain a competitive advantage by reading more books. Check out these eight research-backed reasons why you should make reading a part of your professional development.

1. Reading Increases Professional Opportunities

If you want to give yourself more professional opportunities, then you need to read.

An Oxford University study found that sixteen-year-olds who read books outside of school were more likely to have managerial positions as adults than those who did not read.[2] In this study, researchers analyzed the responses of more than seventeen thousand participants about their extracurricular activities when they were sixteen and their careers at age thirty-three. Interestingly enough, it was participants who read for pleasure in their youth who were more likely to be managers—not those who played organized sports, socialized more, or had greater exposure to the arts.

What is it about reading that's so powerful?

When reflecting upon these results, researcher Mark Taylor said, "The positive associations of reading for pleasure aren't replicated in any other extra-curricular activity."[3] As you'll see throughout the rest of this chapter, reading provides a number of benefits that will help you to learn new skills, improve your people skills, and become a better leader overall.

If you're older than sixteen and worry that you may have missed your opportunity to get ahead by reading books, don't. It's never too late to start reading. The first book I (Jesse) recall reading on purpose was when I was twenty-one.

Reading has been the primary catalyst in my professional development. From working as a retail store manager to working in a call center to serving as a senior marketing manager for one of the world's largest publishing companies to becoming a marketing director for a software startup company, I have found reading to be the single activity that has helped me to progress professionally.

If you start reading (more) now, then you'll be amazed by the professional advancements you can make within the next few years.

2. Reading Improves Your Decision-Making Skills

Every day, you make thousands of decisions. From what you eat and what you wear, to how you get to work and how you respond to the hundreds of emails piling up in your inbox, you make up to thirty-five thousand decisions a day.

For better or worse, many of the decisions we make throughout the day are habitual. We don't give them much thought. They're somewhat automated.

But this isn't the case for many of the decisions we make during our working hours. During these moments, it's important to avoid making ill-informed, impulsive, or snap judgments.

What's the best way to do this? By reading, of course.

Research conducted by a trio of University of Toronto scholars discovered that reading fictional literature "could lead to better procedures for processing information generally."[4] Their research found that people who read fiction developed less of a need for what is called "cognitive closure." In psychology, cognitive closure is a way of saying that we tend to avoid ambiguity and prefer to make definitive decisions, which can lead to poor decision making. This study suggests that reading fictional literature can improve your decision-making ability by reducing your need for making quick—and perhaps irrational—snap judgments.

Reading fiction may help you make better decisions throughout the day, but reading in general will help you make better decisions overall.

As we pointed out earlier, there's a good chance a challenge you're facing has already been addressed in a book. So there's no reason to figure out things on your own if someone else has already solved the same problem. Kick pride to the side. Find a book about a struggle you're facing. And see what you can learn from its author. Chances are you will end up saving yourself a tremendous amount of time and heartache.

3. Reading Reduces Stress

In life, you will have stress. It's not a matter of if but when. And that isn't necessarily a bad thing. Stress is like an alarm your body uses to get your attention focused on whatever situation or challenge you're facing. This is why you need to be ready to manage your stress level well, so you will not allow stress to build up within you like a pressure cooker waiting to explode on whoever is in your path. That's never a good idea.

One of the best ways you can manage your stress level is by reading a book. Recent research found that reading only six minutes per day can reduce your stress level by two thirds.[5] As a stress reducer, reading outperformed listening to music, drinking a cup of tea, and taking a walk.

The next time you feel stressed, instead of reaching for dessert, an alcoholic drink, or an extra serving of food, reach for a book instead. Reading is a powerful antidote to stress. It has an uncanny ability to quickly provide relief, restore peace to your life, and provide you with an ongoing ability to tame your stress.

4. Reading Helps You Sleep

There's a close connection between how well you sleep and your mood. If you're not getting enough rest, then you will most likely feel higher levels of stress. It's a simple equation, when you think about it.

We understand there are times when you will not be able to rest as much as you'd like. But we also believe we have been created with the need to get good sleep at night. Getting a good night's rest is also closely connected to your level of performance on the job. In *Essentialism*, Greg McKeown shares several studies that show sleep is not the enemy of productivity but rather is "a driver of peak performance."[6]

In preparing for a good night's rest, the Harvard Medical School recommends reading as one of the best things you can do.[7] As for me (Jesse), I prefer to keep fiction, biographies, or history books on my nightstand to read at night. These are books I'm not too concerned about dozing off in the middle of the page compared to books I'm reading to learn something specific.

As an aside, if at all possible, don't save the reading you want to do until the end of your day. For example, if you're planning on reading thirty minutes a day, then don't wait until you're lying in bed to accomplish your goal. There's a good chance you'll doze off after a few pages. Instead, set aside books you find *entertaining* for your nighttime reading.

With this in mind, get ready to perform your best tomorrow by turning off your TV, dimming your lights, and reading a book.

5. Reading Improves Your Ability to Lead

Readers fight the stigma of being extreme introverts. People who avoid face-to-face contact for the benefit of immersing themselves in a book. This couldn't be further from the truth.

Reading will improve your people skills. It opens you up to new experiences and gives you the ability to intelligently discuss different ideas and even empathize with people, which is an important leadership skill to possess.

When it comes to understanding other people, one study found that people who read for only thirty minutes a week reported a stronger sense of empathy.[8] Developing the ability to relate to someone else, to really place yourself in his or her shoes, is a skill that will take you a long way in your professional career. Simon Sinek, author of *Leaders Eat Last* and *Start with Why*, believes that possessing the ability to empathize with people "is the most important instrument in a leader's toolbox."[9]

From reading biographies, how-to books, and even fiction, you'll be able to better interact with people, which will help you to become a better leader.

6. Reading Makes You Smarter

Your brain is like a muscle, and you need to exercise it to keep it healthy. Reading is one of the best exercises for providing your brain with a great workout.

When you read, you exercise your brain, which will improve your ability to learn. Think about it this way. In general, if you don't lift weights, then you will not get stronger. Over time, your muscles will become weaker. Now, if you train with weights, then you will be able to improve your strength. The same holds true for your brain. The more you exercise your brain, the better it will perform.

Unlike watching videos, reading boasts a number of intellectual benefits, such as increasing your "vocabulary, general knowledge, and verbal skills."[10] Yes, you can learn new words

PAUL BUYER, PROFESSOR OF MUSIC AT CLEMSON UNIVERSITY, ON THE READING LIFE:

Books have been the single greatest catalyst to my writing, speaking, teaching, and leadership. When I was young, I hated to read and struggled with retention. I had no interest in visiting bookstores and used CliffsNotes to survive high school. But one day while shopping, I saw John C. Maxwell's *The 21 Irrefutable Laws of Leadership* in a store window and decided to pick it up. Once I started reading leadership books, I was hooked and developed an unstoppable hunger to improve and invest in myself. I have now written four books and have a speaking career on the side, in addition to my job as a full professor at Clemson University and a national leader in the Percussive Arts Society.

and ideas by watching videos. But when you compare the word length between the average movie script, which is 7,500 to 20,000 words, to the average length of a novel, which is 80,000 to 150,000 words, then you can quickly see books provide a significantly greater amount of content than movies.

We'll admit that reading is challenging. It is an active process that requires your attention. But fight the resistance, pick up a book, and exercise one of the most important assets you have: your brain.

7. Reading Makes You More Creative

Creativity is an essential characteristic of a modern-day leader. According to a survey of more than fifteen hundred CEOs conducted by IBM, creativity was ranked as the most important leadership skill, which makes perfect sense.[11] The global economy is a complex system, and there are countless interdependent factors that influence both international companies and small businesses in your hometown. To navigate these tumultuous waters, creativity will serve as the North Star of leadership for the foreseeable future. Thankfully, creativity isn't something you're either born with or not—it's something you can develop.

Creativity is more than an unruly force of inspiration reserved for artists who can only hope to harness its power. At its core, creativity does include the ability to come up with original ideas. But it also incorporates the capacity to recognize trends, develop alternative solutions, and mix together different concepts to formulate something new.

According to one study, reading fiction can also help you develop your ability to become more creative. In this study, researchers hypothesized that reading fictional short stories compared to nonfiction essays could enhance creativity, and they assigned one hundred participants either a fictional short story or a nonfiction essay to read. They wanted to see whether or not their exposure to this different material would influence their need for cognitive closure—the desire all of us have to eliminate ambiguity while making decisions.

In the end, they discovered that participants who read the fictional short story had less of a need for cognitive closure, which, according to the researchers, "suggest[s] that reading fictional literature could lead to better procedures of processing information generally, including those of creativity."[12]

This may not be what you want to hear, but consistently reading fiction will fuel your creative abilities as a leader. This doesn't mean you have to read fiction every day. But we do encourage you to serve yourself a side of fictional stories within your reading diet.

8. Reading Improves Your Communication

Developing your ability as a communicator is essential to advancing in your career, leading a team, or building a successful business. Don't read this as a mandate to become a nationally renowned speaker or nail a TEDx Talk at the drop of a hat. All we're saying is improving your ability to express yourself well goes a long way in developing as a leader. We're not alone in this belief. Several studies prove this is the case too.

For starters, according to one poll, the vast majority of employers surveyed (69 percent) said they want to hire people who possess "soft" skills.[13] In other words, employers are interested in hiring people who are able to clearly communicate. Can you express yourself well? Well then, you'll find yourself at the top of a recruiter list soon.

Next, clear communication is essential to building a successful business. Practically speaking, if you're unable to position your services or products well, then you'll create confusion among your potential buyers, which means no one will do business with you. This isn't anecdotal evidence either. Based on one survey, large companies will lose on average $64 million per year and smaller organizations will lose $420,000 annually if they possess inadequate communication.[14]

Finally, to lead a team or company, communication is at the top of the charts when it comes to casting vision, navigating change, or encouraging your team to push toward accomplishing big goals.

Since communication is essential to developing yourself as a leader, make it a priority to read more books. Not because we think you should. But because science—as well as common sense—suggests that reading books will improve your ability to communicate.

How?

According to multiple studies, avid readers possess a larger vocabulary and more fact-based knowledge, which naturally lends itself to communicating better. The more words, concepts, stories, and anecdotes you know, the better you'll be able to communicate clearly, concisely, and compellingly.

Over to You

Are you ready to start reading more books? We hope so.

But before you do, there's one thing you need to know: you cannot read just anything.

If you want to experience the benefits of reading we listed above, then you have to be purposeful in what you read.

Remember, your brain is like a muscle. How you exercise it and what you feed it matters.

If you want to enjoy the benefits of reading, then you need to read often, read broadly, and read beyond your comfort level. A steady dose of comic books and steamy romance novels will not yield the same results as reading classic literature, biographies, and many excellent contemporary nonfiction books.

If you are new to reading, it will take a while to cultivate a taste for good books. It takes time, effort, and practice to get used to reading. The demands of a book far outweigh those of an article from BuzzFeed that's long on headline but short on content.

You have to read books that will enlarge your vocabulary, help you navigate your current circumstances, and equip you with the knowledge you need to make wise decisions. But what books should you read?

That's a great question, and one we cannot answer directly for you. However, we'll walk you through the steps you need to take to choose books that not only interest you but will benefit you the most and help you accomplish your goals.

Further Reading

See firsthand how books have transformed people's lives by reading biographies, including:

Lincoln by David Herbert Donald

The Rise of Theodore Roosevelt by Edmund Morris

The Last Lion (three-book series) by William Manchester and Paul Reid

CHAPTER 3

The Slow Death of Readers

THREE BIG REASONS WHY PEOPLE ARE READING LESS

I find television very educating. Every time somebody turns on the set, I go into the other room and read a book.

Groucho Marx

I (Jeff) know about the slow death of readers all too well. My reading habits suffered in my early adult years when I avoided most learning of any kind. I was so "done" with school that I couldn't wait for the learning stage of life to be over. I know. Dumb, right?

As I look back on this time, I see a twentysomething kid who had few, if any, legitimate goals apart from having a good time. Of all the decades I've lived so far, it's my twenties that serves as the one I'd most appreciate being able to do over.

For me, my twenties were largely a wasted decade—one where I lived for the moment without much if any thought about my long-term future. If this describes you at any point in your life, I'm going to go out on a limb and bet you also did very little reading or learning during this time (except for maybe the "hard lessons" kind of learning).

Making the most of the life you've been given will require a fair amount of intentionality. This doesn't mean you can't spend occasional days, say, surfing the net, bingeing on your favorite Netflix guilty pleasure, or simply taking the day as it comes. Just do those things because you *planned* to do them (and presumably after successfully accomplishing your most important tasks) rather than allowing them to become the default activity any time there is empty space on your calendar.

Jeff's story isn't an isolated case.

As for me (Jesse), I come from the stereotypical West Virginian family, with a coal-miner dad and stay-at-home mom. Education wasn't something encouraged growing up, and applying myself at school or reading for fun or self-improvement wasn't something I started doing until my early twenties.

I passed my English classes in high school by the skin of my teeth, had to take a remedial English course in college, and upon entering graduate school was required to take a remedial writing course—and here I am today, writing a book. I imagine my high school teachers and college professors would do a double take at the thought.

Know what else? Jeff and I are not alone, either.

At one point, we were non-readers. The paths that led us to become non-readers were different. But we were part of a growing trend of non-readers, and to a degree, you're drinking from that same well of influence.

Consider these sobering statistics:

- The number of non-readers in the United States has tripled since 1978.[1]
- Leisurely reading among those fifteen and older has declined 28 percent since 2004.[2]
- Aggregate reading time among Americans has dropped from twenty-three to seventeen minutes per day.[3]
- The number of adults who have not read any books in the past year has increased from 19 percent (2011) to 27 percent (2019).[4]
- Adults in the UK who read one book in the past year dropped from 56 percent (2019) to 51 percent (2020).[5]

These statistics are way more than numbers on a page or a boring math equation. They represent a growing trend in our communities and the people we surround ourselves with. We're pointing this out because we are more than the individual choices we make. Speaking plainly, you are influenced by your friends, family, school, work, and your community—the environment around you. If the environment you live within or the people you surround yourself with don't prioritize reading, there's a good chance you won't either. And this is something you must know.

When you're aware of your surroundings and how they influence you, you can acknowledge them, address them, and then blaze a new path forward. In other words, you can become a reader even if you've always been a non-reader or the people around you don't read.

Let's take a look at some of these influences in turn.

Wealth and Education

Non-readers come in all shapes and sizes. Some don't enjoy reading or prefer to only read online articles. Others don't see the value in reading books. But many non-readers share two common characteristics: a lower level of wealth and education.

Based on a Pew Research Center survey, wealth and education directly correlate to whether or not someone has read a book in the past twelve months.[6] For instance, participants whose annual household income was $30,000 or less were twice as likely to not have read a book in the past year compared to those living in households earning $75,000 or more. What is more, adults with a high school diploma or less are five times as likely to not have read a book in the past year compared to those with a bachelor's degree or higher.

If you fall into either one of these buckets, don't give up hope.

You are not destined to be a non-reader for life.

Regardless of your income, education level, or upbringing, you can read more books, improve your reading comprehension, and experience the professional benefits of reading. Throughout this book, we provide a ton of practical advice you can use to get started today.

If you feel held back by your lack of income, don't.

You don't need regular access to a smartphone, computer, tablet, or e-reader to read books. You also don't need a tremendous amount of disposable income, either. You can borrow books from your local library, family, or friends. Ask for books as gifts. And see if there are any expenses you can replace or reduce to allow investing in books. Whatever path you choose, just know you don't have to be shackled by your income.

Now, if you struggle with reading, you're not alone.

A study by the Program for the International Assessment of Adult Competencies discovered that 35 million US adults read at a fourth-grade level or below.[7] Don't allow shame, embarrassment, or a sense of failure to weigh you down. From your state's education department to resources offered by your local library, there are a variety of free resources available for help.

Fighting for Attention

Can we have your attention, please?

The next big factor behind the decline in reading isn't what you're probably thinking. It's something far less nefarious. And you don't have to look long or hard to find the culprit behind this trend, either. It really boils down to one of the most prized commodities in the world: your attention.

From the number of people who read to the amount of time they read, studies reveal this downward trend began in the 1980s. If you're doing the math, this decline began prior to the proliferation of the internet, smartphones, and social media. So what happened?

What the data indicate is simple: as people began giving more of their attention to watching TV, they slowly devoted less time to reading. Before you jump to false conclusions, we're not saying television is to blame, per se. All we're doing is pointing out that our time is limited to twenty-four hours per day. When we spend time doing anything, whether it is watching TV, scrolling through social media, or exercising, it's gone. For example, if you spend five hours and forty-six minutes per day in front of a TV, computer, smartphone, or tablet—which is the national average—then you will not have time left over for reading.[8] In many ways, the cause of non-readers is really this simple.

There's one more layer to add to this equation: when it comes to your attention, it's in high demand. Businesses both big and small want your attention either to resell it to advertisers or directly promote whatever they're selling. Again, we're not saying this is a bad thing. This business model has been around for hundreds of years (think newspapers, radio, and pamphlets). What we want to point out is that what you choose to give your attention to is one thing—it's another thing to know that your attention is in the crosshairs of corporations. So prepare yourself to be purposeful with your time.

Don't blame TV, social media, or the internet for your being a non-reader. Instead, fight to give your attention to reading more by doing less of whatever else you're giving your leisurely attention to. Your future self will thank you.

Not convinced you should shy away from over-usage of TV, social media, or the internet? Let's take a gander at a few things to change your opinion.

Hello, Digital Age

Pop question: Will spending hours per day watching TV, browsing the internet, or using your smartphone change you in any way?

Time's up.

In short, the answer is yes.

Spending hours per day doing the same thing will influence you as a person. For instance, spending hours per day playing chess, exercising, or playing a musical instrument will boost your performance. Likewise, spending hours per day in front of or engaging with a screen will influence you too, and not in the best of ways.

This isn't a guilt trip. Instead, we want to point out that spending hours per day online will lead to tangible differences in the way you read, focus, and recall information. And this is something you need to know, because if you currently spend hours a day glued to a screen, it will be difficult to transition to reading more books. To a degree, you will experience physical, emotional, and intellectual challenges.

To shine a light on what you're getting into, here are three things you must know as you move toward reading more books.

1. Information Overload

You are swimming in a sea of information. Whether you're at home, at work, in the car, or on your phone, tablet, or laptop, you live in a sea of information. According to the data compiled by Visual Capitalist, in one minute online, 404,444 hours of video are streamed on Netflix, 500 hours of video are uploaded on YouTube, 347,222 stories are shared on Instagram, and 41.7 million messages are shared on smartphones.[9] To be honest, it's really hard to put this in perspective. But there's more to ponder.

There are also 1,761 commercial television stations on the air in the United States[10] and 1.72 billion websites in the world.[11] In 2016 the *Washington Post* published an average of 1,200 stories, graphics, and videos per day, NYTimes.com published 1,605 articles and blog posts per week, and the *Times* published on average 230 pieces of content daily.[12]

Not only is this quantity of content staggering, so too is the information it contains. If you were the average English-speaking person living in the seventeenth century, and you picked up today's edition of the *New York Times*, you would read more information in one issue than you would come across in your lifetime.[13]

Engaging with this amount of information through different devices—like your smartphone, computer, or TV—also has practical effects. When we simply compare how much time we spend with media compared to school, work, family, friends, sleep, and reading books, everything else pales in comparison. As we spend time consuming content and engaging with various types of media, we will inadvertently have less time to spend on anything else. This is why it's essential for us to highlight the amount of media all of us have to deal with. At one point, content was something we had to consciously choose to consume, such as by picking up a newspaper or turning on the radio. However, today it's a way of life.

"Information overload" can lead to stress, anxiety, and indecisiveness, among a host of other things. But that's only part of the problem. Over time, if we spend hours per day consuming media and engaging with electronic devices, we can also run into some other life-changing behaviors, which leads us to the next point.

2. Browsing and Scanning

A few years ago, National Public Radio (NPR) played an epic April Fool's Day prank.

On April 1, 2014, NPR published an article with zero content aptly called "Why Doesn't America Read Anymore?"[14] After the article was shared on social media, commenters came out with guns blazing in the comments, letting the people at NPR know they still read. Well, turns out, the joke was on them. If those overzealous commenters had actually clicked on the article, they would have seen this lovely message: "Congratulations, genuine readers, and happy April Fool's Day!"

Even though this was a hilarious prank, unfortunately, it points to something not funny at all. This joke was played in 2014, and the way people engage with content online today has become far worse. Even assuming someone will actually open an article shared on social media, they may not be reading it anyway.

Consider these statistics:

- Most people spend fifteen seconds or less on a webpage.[15]
- People don't read word-for-word online—they scan.[16]
- Web users scan online in different patterns, including F-Patterns and Pinball Patterns—not linear or line-by-line like a book.[17]
- Most two- or three-letter words are skipped over 75 percent of the time.[18]
- People will read about 20 percent of the text on the average web page.[19]

In addition, information searches online are built to lead us to quickly scan something and move on. Reflecting upon this reality, Nicholas Carr, author of *The Shallows*, said, "It's in Google's economic interest to make sure we click as often as possible. The last thing the company wants is to encourage leisurely reading or slow, concentrated thought. Google is, quite literally, in the business of distraction."[20]

What's our point in sharing this with you?

Reading online will shape the way you read to browse, skip, and scan—not concentrate, read linearly (left to right and start to finish), and dwell on what you're reading. The way you read online is not the way books are intended to be read. If you spend hours every day reading on a smartphone, computer, or laptop, your brain will adapt to reading online—not reading a physical book.

When you pick up a book to read, don't be alarmed if you have trouble at first. There's a good chance it'll take you time to change from the way you've been scanning online to reading a book. One big difference is in your ability to focus for extended periods of time, which leads us to the next point.

3. Attention Span

The staring contest is a game my kids and I (Jesse) play on occasion. The rules are simple: two people stare at each other until one person blinks or looks away. The first person who does this loses.

Now, picture yourself playing a similar game with a goldfish. However, instead of staring at each other you have to focus on one thing. The person (or fish) who loses concentration first loses the game. Do you think you could win? Well, according to one study, you would probably lose to the fish.[21] Gulp.

Here's what you need to know: the digital age has influenced our attention span downward. Basically, it's more difficult today to concentrate on one thing for more than eight seconds. And in saying so, we're not alarmists ringing a conspiracy theory bell, either.

According to a study at the Technical University of Denmark, the collective global attention span is narrowing.[22] Said another way, how much attention we devote to any one thing is dwindling because we have so much information vying for our attention. Commenting on this study, Philipp Lorenz-Spreen said, "Content is increasing in volume, which exhausts our attention and our urge for 'newness' causes us to collectively switch between topics more regularly."[23] When we drink from the fire hose of content, there's only so much we can take.

The amount of information available isn't the only thing making it difficult to focus.

And we have 221 reasons why this is the case.

Based on one survey, the average person carries out 221 tasks per day on their smartphone.[24] When you account for eight hours of sleep, this means you're handling your phone fourteen times per hour. I want to believe that I don't handle my smartphone this often, but I'm having a difficult time convincing myself otherwise. I am the rule and not the exception to consistently checking my phone. And the battle to focus doesn't stop with our phones.

Life is busy.

Personally, I'm married, have five kids, work full-time, participate in the life of our local church, regularly exercise, volunteer as a coach, read books, and write books. Focusing on what's in front of me is challenging. Some days I do well. Other days I fail miserably (you can ask my wife, who often has to redirect me).

I'm not alone in struggling with bad and good distractions. All of us are bombarded with emails, push notifications, text messages, instant messages, advertisements, and (hopefully) pleasant interruptions from family, friends, or colleagues.

Being distracted is more than a nuisance. Distractions pose deadly and practical consequences.

According to one report, approximately nine people are killed and more than one thousand are injured in vehicle crashes in the United States each year because of distracted drivers.[25] And, more practically speaking, it will take you twenty-three minutes and fifteen seconds to return to your original task after being distracted.[26]

So, yeah, swimming in a sea of information and fighting relentless distractions is challenging in general—but a huge obstacle to overcome when reading books. Needless to say, reading a book will be more difficult for you today compared to someone ten or more years ago, because you have to knock down distractions like you're playing whack-a-mole, and you've been training your brain to browse content.

You don't have to oppose technology to read more books. You don't have to trade in your smartphone for a flip phone. You don't have to trash your television or avoid movies. And you don't have to throw away your e-reader.

You can create healthy boundaries with technology and read more books. But there is one caveat: you will have to fight to focus because you live within the digital age. There's really no way around experiencing one of the consequences mentioned above unless you're a strict adherent of digital minimalism or live a life of isolation.

Three Steps to Focus

Thankfully, you can read more books without rejecting technology, throwing away your e-reader, or deleting your apps. In fact, it's not really that complicated. There are only three small steps you will need to take to help yourself focus while you read.

Step 1: Know How You'll Feel

Assuming you fall within the range of screen usage mentioned above, you will experience all sorts of things when sitting down to read a book. From an inability to stay focused to feeling a tinge of anxiety caused by separation from your devices, you won't feel great. So don't be alarmed at this when it happens. Prepare for it to happen.

Step 2: *Reduce Digital Distractions*

You are not a victim of the digital age. You can eliminate digital distractions while you read. This may include leaving your phone in a different room and reading in a space free of any screens.

At first, removing digital distractions is essential to setting yourself up for success. You will be tempted to check your phone or do something else while you read. Being in a place free of anything digital (or whatever distracts you) will help you to fight through distraction temptations.

JEVONNAH ANTWINE ELLISON, HIGH-PERFORMANCE COACH, ON THE READING LIFE:

I have a lot of books around here and I love it that way, because it just reminds me of where I was at a specific point in my life. I can always go back and say, wow, I remember I was going through this when I read that. Or, here's a point that I can apply to how I'm living my life right now. After reading *Digital Minimalism* by Cal Newport and *The Ruthless Elimination of Hurry* by John Mark Comer, I successfully set boundaries with social media. I gave myself a "time block" and "tech check-in days" where I could catch up with social media instead of being connected to it 24/7. Reading these books also prompted me to delete insignificant apps from my phone. I began using technology in a more humane way so that my goals were supported by technology, not controlled by them.

This doesn't mean you can't read e-books. If you prefer e-books, go for it. But when you're reading on a device, be purposeful. Turn off notifications. Move distracting apps on your phone to a different screen. And make whatever changes you need to in order to limit distractions.

Step 3: Make Regular Progress

Reading tweets, scanning online articles, and scrolling through social media is a bad recipe for reading a book. When doing this, you are inadvertently training yourself to have bite-sized concentration and to scan while reading.

Again, don't be surprised that reading books will not be a glorious experience the first time or two. It may take days, weeks, or months to feel good about reading books in any format. This probably isn't what you want to hear, but it's what you need to hear. You see, as you read books, you are rewiring your brain to read from left to right and line by line, which will take time.

Don't be discouraged. Read. Get frustrated. Push through and read again. Get bored. Pick up your book again. In time, you'll feel better about it.

Don't overcomplicate your reading experience. Know you'll face distractions, remove digital distractions, and make a little progress every time you read.

Over to You _____

There are a variety of reasons you may not read as much today as you'd like. It doesn't matter what led you to this point. What matters is that you identify the source of your lack of reading and work toward a solution.

Further Reading

Take a deep dive into this topic:

The Shallows: What the Internet Is Doing to Our Brains
  by Nicholas Carr

Digital Minimalism by Cal Newport

Amusing Ourselves to Death by Neil Postman

CHAPTER 4

The Eight Biggest Reading Excuses Holding You Back

You don't have to burn books to destroy a culture.
Just get people to stop reading them.

Gandhi

Can you read but choose not to?

If so, join the club. There's a big room filled with non-readers. But what's your excuse?

Making excuses is an innate ability all of us possess. From avoiding a tough conversation to choosing not to read, it's tempting to reach into our back pocket and pull out whatever reasons we can muster up. We find something more "important" to do or shift blame onto someone or something else. This way we soften the blow of responsibility and make ourselves feel better.

Granted, all of us make excuses every now and then. But seemingly little excuses can lead to pesky bad habits. As for me (Jesse), I live in the South, and making excuses can be used as a polite way of avoiding someone.

All jokes aside, excuses are crippling. They're like an invisible ball and chain shackling you to whatever is holding you back. Regardless of whether the root of your excuses is fear, avoiding failure, staying comfortable, or a lack of clarity on what to do next, your excuses are like a paralytic force inhibiting you from moving forward.

Excuses will

hamper your personal and professional growth
keep you from accomplishing your goals
sabotage your dreams
inhibit you from reaching your fullest potential

Thankfully, excuses are not permanent or genetic. They're nothing more than a crippling belief or bad habit you can overcome.

If you want to succeed at anything, you'll have to grow in your ability to identify excuses (limiting beliefs) in your life, own them, and take a step outside of your comfort zone. Let us shoot it to you straight: you're not very likely to experience success of any kind if you're not willing to do this. Simply put, people who are successful tend to not make excuses and, instead, do whatever it takes to go through, over, around, or under whatever obstacle they face.

Here's the funny thing about stepping outside of your comfort zone: the more often you do it, the easier it becomes. For example, I (Jeff) used to be terrified of public speaking. Heck, the first time I did an interview on someone else's podcast I experienced a panic attack: my heart raced, I was unable to speak, and I had shortness of breath all at once. Why would anyone want to subject themselves to that a second time? Easy. For me, I knew that sharing my expertise on a podcast or stage was necessary for me to accomplish my goals. So I had a choice to make. I could either buckle down and do the hard thing, or I could decide to be content with not reaching my goals.

You have the same choice every day.

In the words of John C. Maxwell, people "choose the pain of self-discipline, which comes from sacrifice and growth, or they choose the pain of regret, which comes from taking the easy road and missing opportunities."[1] For you, maybe your "pain" was in deciding to read today versus putting it off until later. Yet when you do the hard thing *now* (sacrifice), not only do you avoid the other hard thing later (regret) but something else wonderful happens. It gets easier. And you gradually get better at it.

Just like public speaking, I recognized reading regularly was something necessary for me to do as part of my life's work. I had to be willing to continually learn, grow, and get better. Reading was the fastest, straightest path to make those things a reality.

At first, it sucked. I hated it. I lacked motivation. But doing it regularly, and with a plan in place, not only made reading regularly something that became easier for me to do but gradually turned it into something I really enjoy doing, even something I've become an evangelist for.

That you're reading this book is proof.

In this chapter, we will hand you the keys to unlock yourself from your reading excuses. As you read through the list below, identify what is holding you back, own it, and change it. Rewiring your perspective about reading is not about reading more books, per se. It has more to do with experiencing the transformative effects books provide and becoming the person you want to become—not remaining who you are.

Let's get started.

1. "I Don't Have Time to Read."

This is arguably the most common myth holding people back from reading more books. In an informal email survey we conducted, we asked respondents to describe the most frustrating thing they experience when it comes to reading.[2] Common responses we heard included "I don't have the time to read," "There's usually not enough time in the day," and "I struggle with not having enough time to read." But here's the funny thing about time: we spend it on our priorities.

When we think or utter the words "I don't have the time" with regard to anything we'd like to do more of, in reality we just haven't decided that thing is important enough to pursue. If it were, then we would find the time.

The issue with not having enough time to read is simply this: you've yet to decide that reading is worth making time for. Only once you've made the decision to schedule time for reading, and are willing to protect that time from other interruptions, will it ever have a chance of actually happening.

If you want to read more books, you can.

There's no secret to reading other than making it a priority, picking up a book, cracking it open, and getting to work.

The biggest challenge you will face is yourself. If you want to read more books, then you will have to prioritize reading. There's no way around making this decision, and you're the only one who can make it. Thankfully, even though *you* are the biggest challenge you will face, you are also the answer to your problem in this situation.

We'll admit, there's a bit more to freeing up time to read than meets the eye. That's why we devoted an entire chapter to this conversation. If this is your struggle, then feel free to skip to chapter 6 to slay this dragon.

2. "I Don't Have the Money."

I (Jeff) will be the first to admit that one of the most consistent "complaints" I receive from those listening to my podcast is the money they spend on books. These complaints are in jest, of course. And not one of them has ever uttered a word of regret over the purchases they've made. They realize, like I do, that if just one good idea comes from reading a book, then that's $20-ish well spent.

Books are an investment. Like any investment, you need to spend money. But books are like an investment without the fear of a stock crash—the money you spend will have a return that cannot be taken away.

Books can provide you with new skills, give insight into how to solve a problem, and totally change the course of your life and professional career. This was the case for me (Jesse), and I know that my experience isn't the exception. For one glaring example, Warren Buffett, one of the wealthiest people in the world at the time of this writing, attributes much of his success to a book. "I can't remember what I paid for that first copy of *The Intelligent Investor*," wrote Warren to the shareholders of Berkshire Hathaway.[3] "Whatever the cost, it would underscore the truth of Ben's adage: Price is what you pay, value is what you get. Of all the investments I ever made, buying Ben's book was the best."

Humor us for just a moment: take an inventory of all the things you spend your disposable income on, like lattes, video games, and movies. What's been your return on investment (ROI) for those items? Listen, if it sounds like we're playing hardball, it's because we are. Finding the money to purchase books—books that can change the trajectory of your life and career—isn't that difficult.

Just like finding the time, you may have to decide to give up a handful of things you "need" that really don't belong in the "need" category.

Again, we're not curmudgeons who believe you can't enjoy life and nonessential items. You can. However, some things may need to be put on the back burner in order to make room in your budget for a few good books. In the words of Erasmus, a scholar and philosopher from the fifteenth century, "When I have a little money, I buy books; and if I have any left, I buy food and clothes."[4]

Now, if you're not in a spot to purchase books because of your living arrangements or financial restrictions, don't let that stop you from reading. From getting books from the library to downloading free audiobooks in apps like Libby to borrowing them from your family or friends, there are many creative and free ways you can read or listen to books.

Purchasing a book may not make you a billionaire like Warren Buffett, but building yourself a library is one of the few things that has the potential to make significant returns on the small investments you make in it.

3. "I Don't Like Reading Entire Books."

If this is you, there's a good chance you're not reading the right books for you. If you find that you consistently do not enjoy reading an entire book, you're probably picking out the wrong titles. Selecting a relevant book is something we'll help you figure out in chapter 5.

But we understand this struggle.

When you buy a book, you buy it whole—not in chapters. In general, this lends itself to the belief that you have to read an entire book. But that isn't the case.

Every book you read doesn't need to be read word-for-word. In the words of Sir Francis Bacon, there will be books you taste, others you swallow, and a few you'll chew on and digest.[5] In other words, don't feel obligated to read an entire book—that would be like forcing yourself to watch a terrible movie you rented, only for the sake of getting all the way through it.

If you find something you're reading confusing, not enjoyable, or not beneficial, then you have permission to abandon it with fervor. This is what one respondent to our reading survey is growing to understand. She said, "If a book doesn't speak to me or my unique situation, it's okay to give myself permission not to finish it."

For fiction, if you're not enjoying the story or you're not interested in seeing what happens to the characters, say goodbye to that fictional world. While reading a nonfiction book, if your questions aren't being answered or you're not benefiting, then put it down, cut your losses, and move on.

Talking about nonfiction and business books, here's one great thing to keep in mind: you don't have to read them from cover to cover to discover the essential lessons. Many of these books are written in such a way that every chapter does not build upon the last. Basically, you're not going to miss a critical plot point if you skip or skim a chapter.

Just because you haven't read a book from cover to cover doesn't necessarily mean you can't call it a book you've read. A book is read (i.e., finished) once you're done. This is why we think it's critical for new readers to first decide what they want to get out of a book (the goal) and then determine what amount of reading from the book will be required to reach that goal.

As a rule of thumb, there's an unwritten guideline somewhere that recommends reading at least fifty pages before abandoning a book. This is solid advice for most books. As we'll share in chapter 10, when it comes to reading nonfiction, you can draw most of what you need from the book by using a few reading tips and tricks.

4. "I Don't Know What I Should Read."

To be honest, we don't know what you should read either. Without knowing you—what you like, what you dislike, and what you'd like to learn—it would be nearly impossible to suggest the right book for you.

So, what books should you read? James Clear, author of the hugely popular book *Atomic Habits*, once said, "Read books that are relevant to what you want to achieve and reading will never seem boring."[6] For many, part of the problem of committing to reading is boredom. If that's consistently the case for you, you're choosing the wrong books. As James suggested, ask yourself what it is you want to achieve. What do you desire to learn more about? Is there a skill you've been longing to acquire?

At various times in my life, I (Jeff) have been in situations where I wanted or needed to learn more about things like social media marketing, public speaking, internet marketing, and more. Each time, I found every aspect of the reading process fun because I determined what I wanted to achieve first before even buying a particular book.

From researching books on a particular topic and choosing which ones to purchase to receiving the books in the mail and diving into them, I've found that being more intentional with what you're choosing to read makes all the difference in the world.

The books I buy, I buy on purpose and with intention. That means that when it comes time to begin reading, my motivation is built right in.

Still unsure what you should read? Hang tight. We'll get there in chapter 5.

5. "I Don't Read Fast Enough."

Says who? Compared to who? Who cares!

This concern is one I (Jeff) once possessed, but not anymore. I had to finally admit that it just doesn't matter. Nowhere is it written that you should read at a certain pace. There's no measuring stick.

Personally, my reading habit involves a great deal of pausing in order to take notes. I often spend time in thought, pondering a particular passage or imagining myself actually applying the principle in some way. For example, I recently spent nearly four hours with a book that was only "supposed" to take about two hours to finish.

Reading isn't all about how fast you can read or about finishing a book, and it's certainly not all about finishing within the average time a particular book *should* take. Reading books is more about becoming a better human—this is the beauty of books.

In this book, we'll show you how to measure your reading speed and share ways you can increase it. But this is to help you improve your ability to read—not so you can measure up to some sort of universal reading speed standard.

Give yourself permission to compare your reading speed and ability only to yourself. Sure, there are reading speed averages, as studies have observed. But like any average, this means some people read slower than the average and others read faster.

If you don't want to blow through a book, great. Take the time you need to read, ponder, and act upon whatever you read (or listened to).

As mentioned, I prefer to pause and ponder while reading. Giving myself permission to stop and start in this way has led me to enjoy reading that much more. As for Jesse, he has a practice of reading an entire book, making marks along the way, and then going back through it afterward to take down more comprehensive notes.

When it comes to reading books, get an idea of where you're at and strive to improve yourself compared to who you were yesterday—not anyone else. You have permission to read and reflect in whatever way works best for you.

6. "I Only Like to Listen to Audiobooks."

We love audiobooks, and listening to them has been a part of our reading diet to varying degrees for years. As for me (Jeff), early in my reading journey, audiobooks were a lifesaver. They were one way I could take something I dreaded—my commute to work—and turn it into something I looked forward to. In taking a cue from Zig Ziglar, I turned my commute into an "automobile university."[7]

So, should you read physical books or listen to audiobooks? Well, it depends.

For starters, books and audiobooks are different. We're not saying one is superior to the other or that you should choose one over the other. Choosing between a physical book and audiobook is similar to choosing between watching a movie based on a book or reading the book itself. It all depends on what you want to experience and get out of it. You have to know the differences between them and which option best suits your needs.

For starters, physical books lend themselves to better reading comprehension and retention of difficult texts (the key word here is *difficult*). According to one study, students who listened to a podcast lesson performed significantly worse on a quiz compared to students who read the same lesson on paper.[8] But when it comes to general reading comprehension—for example, a book you're reading for pleasure or insight—one study found participants who listened to the text received similar reading comprehension scores compared to those who read the text.[9]

Interested in entertainment? Read or listen to a book. In a book club? Both options work. Multitasking or commuting to work? Audiobooks are a clear winner here. Need to study something? We'd suggest picking up a physical book and possibly supplementing your reading with the audiobook.

If listening to audiobooks meets your needs and it's the only way you can consume books right now, go for it. Don't let anyone else tell you otherwise—they're only being pretentious if they do.

7. "I Find It Difficult to Read for More Than Five Minutes."

"Look! Squirrel!"

We get it—staying focused isn't easy. From the temptation to check our smartphones a dozen or more times per hour to work, social media, family and friends, and everything in between, it's a Herculean task to focus on anything. Actually, a study conducted by Microsoft in 2015 found that the average human attention span in 2013 was a whopping eight seconds. To put this in perspective, goldfish have an average attention span of nine seconds.[10]

So, yeah, if you don't consider yourself a reader today, it will be difficult for you to push through the initial pages, and here's why: reading is something you do. Of course, we're stating the obvious. But we want to emphasize this point because reading is an active process, and as we share in chapter 9 about good reading habits, limiting your distractions is one big leap you can take toward focusing on what you read.

At first, don't be surprised when—not *if*—you don't feel like reading, are easily distracted, or find it difficult to read for extended periods of time. Create for yourself a good reading environment and prepare to push through these internal battles. You can thank us later.

8. "I Cannot Learn from Books."

This is a tough nut to crack, and there are three potential ways to overcome this excuse.

First, this technically may be the case for you. If you possess a reading disability (e.g., dyslexia) or struggle with written language (e.g., grammar), then yes, it will be difficult for you to learn from books. This doesn't mean you lack intelligence—far from it. All this means is that you have a problem that can be improved in most cases with training or professional help.

I (Jesse) have two sons who have dyslexia. Both of them have participated in specialized reading tutoring, and both of them have made significant strides in improving their ability to read. This doesn't mean their condition went away. What happened over the course of time and training is that they learned new ways to read and comprehend in light of their condition.

Second, reading is a science, and it's something you have to learn. For instance, if you missed or failed language arts classes in school (like I did), then learning from reading will be tough at first because you lack the tools you need to comprehend and retain what you're reading. Thankfully, this is a gap in knowledge you can fill. And in time, with practice

LIZ WISEMAN, AUTHOR OF SEVERAL BOOKS INCLUDING *MULTIPLIERS* AND *THE MVP MINDSET*, ON THE READING LIFE:

For me, the value of reading comes less from what it prompts us to do and far more from how a book changes the way we think. Reading books allows us to see the world through another person's mind. Like a great mentor, we can borrow someone else's brain and look at the world through their lens. When we read books written by great thinkers, it allows us to reach higher. I see it much like "Rent the Runway" for your mind, working the way Rent the Runway allows someone to rent an expensive designer gown and get to wear something more expensive than what they could otherwise afford. Reading books allows us to think beyond our current knowledge and try on mindsets that are perhaps more evolved or intentionally developed than our own. Reading is how we challenge our current thinking and see beyond our echo chambers. I think it helps us expand our minds and question ourselves.

or perhaps with professional help if needed, you'll be better able to learn from what you read.

Finally, there are some who don't possess any sort of limitations or lack of knowledge but have said, "I don't learn from books" as an excuse not to read. If you're reading this book, that's probably not the case for you. But keep what we shared here in mind as you talk to or encourage non-readers to read.

Over to You

Did you find the excuse holding you back?

Great; now it's time to address it and move on.

Be patient as you tackle whatever it is. It may take more time than you think to resolve whatever you're going through. So own your excuse and take responsibility, and you'll be well on your way to becoming a lifelong reader before you know it.

Further Reading

Be inspired to overcome your challenges and excuses:

The Obstacle Is the Way: The Timeless Art of Turning Trials into Triumphs by Ryan Holiday

The Autobiography of Benjamin Franklin by Benjamin Franklin

Walt Disney: An American Original by Bob Thomas

PART 2

THE BOOKS YOU NEED TO READ

CHAPTER 5

Six Ways to Know What You Should (and Shouldn't) Read

*If we encounter a man of rare intellect,
we should ask him what books he reads.*

Ralph Waldo Emerson

Phil Knight, the cofounder of Nike, keeps his personal library behind closed doors. Today, it is a thing of legend. It is located in a room behind his formal office at the Nike headquarters. Not many have entered this sacred room. If you were granted permission to enter, you'd have to remove your shoes and honor his collection of books by bowing. When asked if his library still remains, Phil replied, "Of course the library still exists. I'm always learning."[1]

The great lengths Phil has taken to protect his library may sound a bit eccentric.

But are they really?

The books you read will become a part of your life. They will inform who you are—your faith, knowledge, and values.

Perhaps this is what Ralph Waldo Emerson had in mind when he said, "I cannot remember the books I've read any more than the meals I have eaten; even so, they have made me."[2]

Most of us, including ourselves, don't have the resources to build a multimillion-dollar library. But we can all collect books to read today, tomorrow, or never. Books that will help us to become a better man or woman, son or daughter, mom or dad, friend, employee, or entrepreneur. Books that will inspire us to great heights. Books that will help us to overcome whatever challenge we're facing. And books that will help us to accomplish our goals.

What we're saying is more than a bunch of hooey. One study discovered that children in homes of families with a personal library read better than their peers and were more likely to complete college.[3] This study didn't only observe über-wealthy families, either. We're talking about families with a hundred books or so in their home. Why is this the case? Well, it turns out if you are devoted to educating yourself, you will influence your children to do the same.

This shouldn't surprise you after reading chapter 2. The benefits of reading and surrounding yourself with books will be a significant boost to your personal development, influence, and career. The books in your collection will (and should) be different from what's in someone else's library. They'll be a reflection of who you are and a map leading you to where you're going.

In this chapter, we're going to help you build a personal library. We're not going to talk about what type of bookshelves you should purchase or how you should organize your books. We're going to walk you through the books you should read—and what books you shouldn't read.

1. Read for Personal Change

Before you can lead effectively, before you can effect change, and before you can ever expect to leave your mark on your community, your company, and the world, you must lead yourself first. Wouldn't it be great if you had an instruction manual showing you how? Well, thankfully, you do. But it's not just one manual—it's a lot of manuals in the form of books.

As we've pointed out, books are powerful. Their pages possess the ability to make you smarter and more creative and to help you become a better leader and person. In an interview with the *New York Times*, President Obama shared how rediscovering reading in college led him to rebuild himself. He said reading "introduced him to the power of words as a way to figure out who you are and what you think, and what you believe, and what's important."[4] Regardless of where you're at in life, what shortcomings you want to overcome, or what strengths you want to build upon, books can help you get there.

"Self-awareness for $200, Alex."

If I (Jeff) had a nickel for every time I was deep inside a book on personal and professional development and recognized an area of my life that needed work—well, I'd have a lot of nickels.

In reading for personal change, you are embarking on a reading journey with the express purpose of discovering more about yourself and what makes you tick. At first, read books that cover personality types, mindsets, and leadership styles. Before building your life up, there are times you have to dig down to lay a foundation. So take the time to examine yourself in order to better understand who you are, in all of your warts and glory.

Reading books for personal change is not confined to the self-help aisle, either. Your life can be influenced for the better by any type of book. It can be an insightful sentence you read. A fictional story that shed light on something you're going through. A person from the past you connected with through reading their biography. Don't limit yourself to self-help books. Be open to experiencing a new perspective from anything you read.

To discover books for personal change, ask yourself,

1. *Am I aware of my strengths, weaknesses, talents, or leadership style?* Assess yourself by picking up books that will guide you in examining yourself.
2. *What quality or virtue do I want to develop?* Find a book about someone who exemplifies this characteristic or books on how to develop the virtues you aspire to possess.
3. *Who inspires me?* See if this person has written a book, or read a book about this person.
4. *What type of work do I want to do?* Read books about the work you're interested in to better understand what interests you about this line of work.

2. Read for Personal Enrichment

Reading doesn't always have to be a task you complete. And it doesn't have to be directly related to a goal you want to accomplish or a skill you want to learn, either. Reading can be something you do for the pleasure of reading itself.

Do you enjoy dystopian fiction? Explore a world oppressed by a political state or overrun by zombies to experience a different perspective on contemporary issues. Love a particular genre of music? Get carried away by authors who explore the history and formation of your favorite music or tell tales about famous musicians. Have a favorite hobby? Pick up books that will help you better understand what you like and look for stories that include characters who also enjoy this hobby. Interested in a particular era in history, news story, or world event? Or do you want to read a book because you just like it? Go for it.

The benefits you can experience when reading books are not directly tied to nonfiction or how-to books. As a general rule of thumb, reading books will enrich your life in many ways—so enjoy the books you like for the sake of the books themselves.

To find books you'll love, ask yourself,

1. *What types of stories do I love?* Discover new authors and titles by exploring books similar to something you've read before.

2. *Do I really like a particular genre of music, musician, or band?* Get biographies or books about the history of the music you like.

3. *Do I have one or more hobbies?* Buy books about the hobbies you possess or want to learn about.[5]

4. *What historical event or person interests me the most?* Get one or more books about the era itself and at least one biography about the person you'd like to learn more about.

3. Read for Spiritual Enlightenment

"Why am I here?"

This is a common question that's probably been asked by every man, woman, and child since the beginning of time.

When pursuing the answer to this question, most people seek it through religious, supernatural, or spiritual ways. Regardless of whether you are seeking the answer to this question or rekindling what you believe, there are several genres of writing you can explore.

For starters, most religions have a sacred text or texts—source material they use as the standard to guide their beliefs and practices. Examples include the Bible for Christians, the Qur'an for Muslims, and the Tripitaka for Buddhists. If you want to know what a religion believes, it's best to read their source materials.

As for me (Jesse), I make it a practice to regularly read the Bible and also read it with my family. I'm far from doing this daily. But I try. Reading the Bible has a way of reconnecting me to my faith and what I believe and guiding me in the life I live and the decisions I make.

One common genre many authors use to share their beliefs is nonfiction—in particular, instruction, self-help, and biography. With self-help books, authors distill practical lessons from religious texts or philosophy into bite-sized literary morsels. In this way, they focus on instructing or exemplifying "how to" live out a particular belief. Think *The Obstacle Is the Way* by Ryan Holiday, about stoicism, or *Knowing God* by J. I. Packer, on Christianity.

Biographies can give you a glimpse into the life of someone who lived out their faith. These snapshots paint one picture of how to live out your religious beliefs. In a way, they help you to see by example how someone else lived their life, which can be a great encouragement. Nonfiction religious books are helpful when it comes to "how to" live out your life based on these beliefs. But there's one weakness these books tend to have, which leads us to the next genre.

Fiction based off of religious texts is another powerful way authors can share their religious beliefs. Through their works, you can explore common themes of religion. Two popular fiction writers who come to mind are C. S. Lewis and J. R. R. Tolkien. Lewis incorporated many Christian themes throughout his children's fantasy series, The Chronicles of Narnia. As for Tolkien, he explored Christian themes from a Catholic perspective in the three volumes of *The Lord of the Rings* without many direct references. Without taking religious fiction as gospel, you can experience how these authors express their faith through their writing, which is one way you can rekindle your affections, values, and beliefs.

As you think about the answer to this question, be sure to read books on this topic. As for me (Jesse), I enjoy regularly reading the Bible and Christian nonfiction books, and I even graduated from a Christian seminary, which is theological graduate school. Pursuing graduate studies isn't for everyone, nor is it required. But we do encourage you to include religious books in your pursuits to help you discover why you're here.

To find books for spiritual enrichment, ask yourself,

1. *Am I interested in a specific religion?* Purchase the sacred text about that religion or a book about that religion itself.
2. *Who are two or three pastors, theologians, or philosophers I'm familiar with?* Get a book they've written, a book explaining their work, or a biographical work about them.
3. *Do I have questions about life, faith, or some other topic related to my spirituality?* Buy two or more

books on that topic from different perspectives to consider the answers to your questions from different points of view.

4. Read for Professional Development

Reading in general will help you to develop yourself personally and professionally. But reading books relevant to your line of work or ways you want to grow can help you to sharpen yourself and stay ahead of the game.

Interested in learning a new skill? Purchase a how-to book or read a biography on someone who's considered an expert in that field. Have a burning desire to share a message? Get a book on public speaking or study someone known for their oratory skills. Preparing for a certification? See if there's a book you can read on the topic.

When it comes to picking books for professional development, take time to reflect on your work, your next step, and what you need to know or experience to get there.

Here's the two-step process we recommend: first, break down your field into the smallest segments possible. For example, if you want to pursue a career in marketing, the first thing you'll want to do is divide marketing into smaller categories (e.g., social media marketing, branding, copywriting). If you need help, ask some friends, your boss, or a mentor or just do a search online. Taking this step will help you to better focus your reading.

Second, identify what skills you need to master and what related information you need to know. Generally speaking, many fields have multiple disciplines you can master within them. From specializing in a specific field of medicine to mastering a particular programming language, there are potentially countless rabbit trails you can pursue. Unless you're a polymath with the ability to master several different fields, it's best to focus on learning a few things while informing yourself of whatever else you just need general knowledge of.

Picking back up on our example of marketing, let's say you wanted to master content marketing and SEO. In this case, you'd want to spend most of your available time (80 percent) studying and experimenting in these two fields. With your remaining time, focus on developing relevant knowledge as well as foundational skills, such as data and analytics, behavioral psychology, and copywriting to create a well-rounded understanding in your field.

Taking these two steps will make it easier for you to laser-focus on what you need to read for professional development.

DAN MILLER, *NEW YORK TIMES* BESTSELLING AUTHOR, ON THE READING LIFE:

I have books like *Think and Grow Rich* where the original book probably cost me about $4. But the impact on my life? There's just no way to quantify that. So I can't really connect the dots because there's so much that overlaps. The quantity of books that I read, and have read, and the pieces in each of those give me the opportunities that I experience today. It's not just things we can quantify mathematically. The life experience that I have, the fullness of the life that I have, the rich relationships that I have, are also a result of reading. And those, we can't really quantify tangibly financially, but it is the ROI of reading.

To find books for your professional development, ask yourself,

1. *What's a skill I want to develop?* Look for a how-to book on this skill or find a book about someone who possesses this skill.
2. *Who is someone I admire in my line of work?* Get a book written by this person or a book about them.
3. *Do I need to develop as a leader?* Purchase books about leadership or books about leaders you respect.

5. Read for Wisdom

Gaining wisdom is a lifelong pursuit. We hate to say it, but on this side of the grave, you'll never "arrive." It's impossible to know everything, and there will never be a time in life where you will not need the insight from someone else on whatever you're going through—even if it's found in a book.

Reading books about historical events (local, regional, national, and world), people, and movements is essential to making sense of your life and the events shaping you today. You were born into a moment in history that was shaped by everything that took place before you arrived. And though everything that happened up to your birth was outside of your control, it influences who you are—and so does everything going on around you today.

When you walk into the past through books and meet the people and events who shaped where you live, your work, and the systems that influence you, like economics and government, you'll be better able to walk the path of life laid out before you.

To find books to grow in wisdom, ask yourself,

1. *Where did I grow up?* Find books about the town or area you're from to shed light on how these communities may have influenced you and your family.

2. *What events have influenced me and my family the most?* Get books on these events from different perspectives; that way you'll develop a well-rounded understanding.

3. *What's a current issue I'm concerned about or interested in?* Get a few books about this issue to explore it from a perspective you agree with and one you disagree with to obtain a well-rounded point of view.

4. *Who's a famous politician, businessperson, author, musician, pastor, philosopher, or military figure I'm interested in?* Purchase one book about someone you admire to see what you can learn from their life and experiences.

6. Read Recommended Books

Reading a book recommended by someone you know or respect from a distance can be a game-changer. As we've said time and time again, books inform who we are as a person.

If a book changed someone else's life and they recommend it, get it. Every one of us—including you—has been or will be influenced by a book. You may not experience the same level of transformation they proclaim, but there's a good chance you'll at least benefit in some way from reading it.

To find the best book recommendations, explore books recommended by people you admire. If you know them personally, great. This step is easy. Just ask them what books changed their life, made a significant difference to them, or helped them with something you're interested in knowing.

To find book recommendations from people you admire from a distance, see if they've shared any online. If this doesn't work out, then don't be afraid to hit them up on social media, send them an email, or connect with them at an event. You may not get an answer. But don't let that stop you from at least trying.

If you come up empty-handed in your quest for book recommendations, you can always search online for the "best" books on whatever topic you're interested in exploring. Read a few of these lists. See what books make the same lists in different publications. Then pick the one that sounds most interesting to you.

Countless books have made countless changes in people's lives. And that can be true for you too. So make a list of people from whom you'd like to know what books they've read. Find them. Buy them. Devour them. And enjoy whatever they have to offer you.

To find recommended books, ask yourself,

1. *Has someone I admired up close or from a distance recommended books to read?* If not, consider reaching out to this person for book recommendations—even if you don't think they'll respond.
2. *Has a media company I follow, such as CNN, Fox News, or Forbes published a must-read list?* See what books they suggest reading.
3. *What about a media company I don't agree with?* Expand your horizons by reading a recommended book from their list.

4. *What are my favorite books?* Find two to four titles similar to your favorite books by leveraging the search capabilities of an online bookstore—or ask a knowledgeable bookstore employee or librarian.

5. *Have I read any books about my profession?* Search for a list of the "best" books about your profession or business from a reputable source.

6. *What books have won awards or been bestsellers in my desired area of study?* Read through lists of Pulitzer Prize, Nobel Prize, or National Book Award winners and bestseller lists like those published by the *New York Times* and *Wall Street Journal.*

Over to You

Don't feel overwhelmed by the number of books available.

Take the time you need to think about what you should read. Assuming you're taking a step toward reading more, park yourself on this chapter for a moment. Identify what books will benefit you the most and books you'll enjoy reading for the sake of reading. Spending time here will save you wasted time in the future and put you well on your way to living a reading life—and confidently saying no to tens of millions of books.

Further Reading

As you build your library, be sure to check out *The Black Swan* by Nassim Nicholas Taleb for an introduction to building an anti-library, which is a library full of books you haven't read and may never read.

CHAPTER 6

Too Busy Not to Read

NINE WAYS TO FREE UP MORE TIME TO READ

> Employ your time in improving yourself by
> other men's writings so that you shall come easily
> by what others have labored hard for.
>
> *Socrates*

Being busy isn't necessarily a badge of honor.

Busyness can give you a sense of importance. But you could be busy doing the wrong things or too many things, or because you're mismanaging your schedule.

Busyness can also be a season of life. For me (Jesse), juggling responsibilities between work, family, volunteering, involvement in our local church, and reading and writing is tough. To be honest, oftentimes I just have to prioritize as best as I can and white-knuckle through the day.

Regardless of your reason for busyness, don't allow your schedule to dictate your priorities or stop you from reading. The scientific benefits alone are worth the effort to make reading a priority.

Thankfully, this won't be as difficult as you think. There are several easy ways you can free up time in your schedule to prioritize reading.

1. Reading Doesn't Take as Long as You Think

Physical books look daunting. Many books exceed hundreds if not thousands of pages and can weigh a couple of pounds, and seeing them makes you realize reading isn't child's play—it's work. Even though books can appear intimidating, they don't take as long to read as you might think.

In chapter 9, we share how you can test and improve your reading speed measured by how many words per minute (wpm) you can read. For the sake of proving our point about how long it takes to read a book, let's assume your reading rate is similar to the average rate for adults who read in English, which is 238 wpm for nonfiction books and 260 wpm for fiction.[1] Now, many nonfiction books are about 50,000 words long—including this book. So if you divide 50,000 by 238, you can see that it will take you 210 minutes (or 3.5 hours) to read an average-length nonfiction book, which isn't bad at all.

We understand these numbers may still feel vague to you, so let's take a look at the average reading time of a few books and series to help you get the picture:

- The Harry Potter series: 4,555 minutes
- The Bible: 3,312 minutes
- *The Lord of the Rings* trilogy: 1,987 minutes
- *Pride and Prejudice*: 509 minutes
- *Read to Lead*: 220 minutes

- *The Giver*: 183 minutes
- *The Alchemist*: 164 minutes

We want to make sure you let this point sink in for a moment. Assuming your reading speed is average, it will take you less than four hours to read the average nonfiction book. To take this one step further, let's say you read for thirty minutes every day. At this rate, you could read one nonfiction book per week and fifty-two books per year.

Reading more books isn't a luxurious pastime reserved for the independently wealthy. Reading more books is something you can find the time to do. Let us show you how.

2. Commit to Making Reading a Priority

Don't skip this part. Don't read ahead to get the tactics. Don't worry about learning the reading hacks—yet. There's one thing you must do first.

To find the time to read, you'll first have to commit to reading. Reading is something you must commit to. Freeing up your time without making this commitment is like trying to take a cross-country road trip without any gas: you won't get far.

You are the only person who can make this commitment. We can't do it for you. Your family, friends, mentor, manager, or significant other cannot force you to do this. You have to own this decision and make it happen.

When you decide to prioritize reading, then, come what may, you'll find the time to crack open a book. Whatever we prioritize, we find the time to do—including reading books.

Chapter 7 takes you through the steps you need to take to prioritize your reading goals. Read that chapter. Review your goals. Let the vision of who you want to become and what you want to read be the fuel you need to commit to reading books, learning new skills, and boosting your career.

Ready to commit to reading more books? Great. Before finding ways to free up your time, it's best to review your daily and weekly rhythms first.

3. Review Your Life's Rhythms

Before equipping yourself with productivity hacks, the best thing you can do is to track your time. We'll be honest: this is tedious and not a whole lot of fun. But tracking your time is arguably the best thing you can do to find time to do anything.

When you reflect upon your daily and weekly rhythms, you'll get a clear picture of how you're spending your time. From spotting potentially countless times you check your smartphone to watching television, tracking your time is like holding up a mirror to your life. You'll clearly see how you're actually spending your time—not how you *think* you are.

What is more, when you really see where your time goes, you'll feel more compelled to own how you're spending it. As you track your time, before you commit to doing something, you'll naturally feel a sense of ownership and question whether or not you want to do whatever you set your heart on doing.

This isn't some sort of pop-psychology hack, either. The benefits of tracking your time are similar to journaling what you eat for the sake of losing weight. Multiple studies have confirmed how keeping an accurate food log is nearly a sure-fire way people can lose weight. Journaling helps you to see and take responsibility for what you eat—or what you do with your time.

Reflect upon your daily and weekly rhythms. Listen to your life. Be transparent with how you're spending your time. Look for ways you can make the time to read.

4. Slay the Most Common Distraction

If you're still finding it difficult to find the time to read, here are several common time-suckers you can avoid to create more margin in your life:

- The average US adult spends an average of forty-two minutes per day on Facebook.[2]
- The average daily time spent on YouTube is forty minutes.[3]
- On average, US adults consume five hours of TV per day.[4]
- The average worker spends forty-six minutes commuting to and from work (audiobooks, anyone?).[5]

For the sake of emphasis, there's one time-sucker in particular we want to highlight: your smartphone. It is arguably one of the greatest distractions you'll face. As a smartphone user, you're carrying in your pocket a digital vortex that can act like an irresistible force occupying your time and attention. According to a survey of eleven thousand smartphone users, RescueTime found the average person spent three hours and fifteen minutes per day on their phone.[6] This

Go to readtoleadbook.com/resources to download a time tracking journal.

isn't an isolated study, either. Many other surveys and studies have discovered similar smartphone usage numbers. To drive home the point, this means the average US adult will spend nearly one day per week on a smartphone, and roughly fifty-three days per year scrolling, browsing, or whatever else on a mobile device.

Thankfully, we don't have to rely on surveys to see how often we use a mobile device. Depending on what smartphone you own, you can use the screen time feature to see how much time you spend on your device. If you have this feature, take a moment to look at your screen time and, for better or worse, let that sink in.

We're not saying you cannot watch TV or funny cat videos, or spend time with your friends on social media. If you are spending time doing what you want to do, that's okay. But if you want to better yourself professionally, then we encourage you to audit your life, see where you may be wasting time, and be purposeful with what you read. You'll thank us later.

KARY OBERBRUNNER, BESTSELLING AUTHOR OF *UNHACKABLE, THE ELIXIR PROJECT,* AND *DAY JOB TO DREAM JOB,* ON THE READING LIFE:

I think the person who does not read is living arrogantly. A person who says "I don't need to read" or "I don't want to read" is basically saying to themselves, "I don't need to think." In other words, "Everything that I already have in my head is sufficient. I'm not willing to be open. I'm not willing to read things that will challenge, that will upset, that will disrupt. I'm good."

5. Replace Something

Like anything in life, if you want to start something new and accomplish a goal, then you'll most likely have to cut back on something else. If you're currently not reading as many books as you'd like to, then you'll have to reprioritize your schedule to make it happen.

When it comes to reading more, don't assume you can simply add a new to-do to your daily schedule and get it done. Trust us. It won't happen.

After you review your life's rhythms, we'll wager you'll be able to identify one or more ways you waste time. From watching too much television, staying up late, and sleeping in to checking your mobile device multiple times per hour, there's bound to be at least one hole in your schedule where time pours out, never to return.

Instead of trying to add an additional item to your schedule, replace something you're already spending your time on with reading books. For starters, look closely at your media consumption and smartphone usage. Trade fifteen or thirty minutes of your daily time spent watching television or messing with your smartphone with time spent reading a book.

Tend to scroll social media while eating your breakfast? Flip through a few pages of a book instead. Do you veg out aimlessly in front of a TV after work or before you go to sleep? Relax and reduce your stress levels with a book you'd love to read. Waiting fifteen minutes in line to pick up your kids from daycare or school? Put down your phone and pick up a book. Wander around on the weekends? Binge-read books.

Over the years, my (Jesse's) desire has waned for keeping up with the football season, blockbuster hits, or the latest TV shows. As I've increased my consumption of books, my palate for what I want out of life has gradually changed. Today, instead of watching something during the day and at night when I feel like checking out, I generally pick up a book instead. I also read out loud to my wife at night, which is the perfect way to relax before going to bed.

There's no one-size-fits-all approach to replacing something in your schedule with reading books. But we know you can at a minimum score fifteen to thirty minutes of reading time every day by replacing time you'd normally spend on your smartphone or in front of a television.

6. Fight Tech with Tech

Yes, this does sound ironic. But here's the deal: it's difficult to put down your phone or stop consuming inordinate amounts of media cold turkey. Changing any habit after months or years of practicing it isn't easy. Besides, plenty of studies indicate that screen time and social media can have addictive elements. So you can't necessarily just put things down.

But you're not alone in your battle to reduce your smartphone usage or screen time.

You can fight technology with technology.

Spend too much time during work on your laptop or desktop browsing social media or news sites? Download an extension to block you from visiting those pages. Distracted by social media apps, games, or news apps on your smartphone? Download an app to block you from opening them during certain times. Spend too much time streaming TV shows and movies? Use a device to set a time to shut off your Wi-Fi.

Remember, you do not have to be a slave to technology. You can replace the time you spend on or in front of any device with reading a book. At the end of the day, you'll have to choose to put down your smartphone, unplug your TV, or turn off your Wi-Fi. Of course flipping the switch or pulling the plug will not completely sever your screen time once and for all. But it will empower you today to replace some of your time spent on a phone or screen with reading a book.

7. Schedule Your Ideal Day and Week

To make time to read, to make it a habit you want to "install," there's one more thing you must be willing to do: get comfortable with the idea of scheduling time to read. This means putting it on your calendar and treating the time with the same level of importance you'd give to any other can't-miss meeting or appointment.

However, if you haven't reflected on how you spend your time every day and throughout the week, this step will not work well. Without the knowledge of how you spend your time, you will not be able to set realistic goals.

Scheduling your ideal day and week boils down to two things: clarifying your reading goals and scheduling time to read. First, learn more about setting reading goals in chapter 7. Depending on your annual reading goal, break this down into monthly, weekly, and then daily reading goals.

Second, figure out how much time it'll take you to read the book you want to read that week, then schedule that time in your calendar. For the sake of argument, let's say

Go to readtoleadbook.com/resources for a list of up-to-date apps and devices you can use to block apps, Wi-Fi, and more.

you decided to read a book that'll take you three and a half hours. When making your schedule, you can block off thirty minutes every day during the week or you can read for one or two hours on one or two different days. Whatever you do, add reading to your calendar.

It doesn't matter how you schedule your reading time. It just matters that you make room in your calendar to do so. The only thing we caution against at first is scheduling hours of reading time in one day if you're not used to reading that much. Trying to bite off more than you can chew is one way to choke on fulfilling your reading goals.

8. Say No When You Know You Say Yes Too Often

Scheduling time to read is like making an appointment with yourself. It's a critical time you'll spend on your personal and professional development. So don't treat this time lightly by skipping or canceling it on a whim.

When someone asks if you're available during a time you've scheduled to read, resist the temptation to look at your calendar, see their request *only* conflicts with your reading time, and say, "Sure, I can meet then." Easily giving up on the time you've scheduled for yourself is a trap. Watch out for it.

Let go of the guilt of saying no. Allow "No" to be a complete sentence. You're not obligated to defend it.

In his incredibly useful book *Gettin' (un)Busy: 5 Steps to Kill Busyness and Live with Purpose, Productivity, and Peace*, Garland Vance writes that many of us say yes too quickly and too often.[7] We "default to yes," and if we do say no, we feel as if we need to defend our answer. "Defending no opens the door for the person who's asking to challenge your reasons or to solve the problem your reasons impose."

Garland goes on to suggest you should default to no and defend (to yourself) your *yeses*.

Don't get me (Jeff) wrong. Life is full of moments when we need to forgo scheduled plans because our help or our time is legitimately needed elsewhere. But more often than not, setting aside time for requests like these is completely within our control.

When a request for a meeting, a phone call, or whatever comes up during your scheduled time to read, and it's not an emergency, don't give up without a fight. Suggest another time. It's as simple as saying, "I have an appointment then. Would such-and-such time work for you?" An appointment with yourself is still an appointment.

9. Make Time to Read throughout the Day

The key to reading books is to make the time to read. Reading more isn't something that will happen by accident. Sure, there's a chance you'll read more books when your desire to read grows strong enough. Other times, you'll have to discipline yourself to read even if you don't feel like doing it at the moment. In these cases, your feelings will follow later.

There are a ton of productivity hacks and systems you can follow. But there's only one way you can make the time to read, and that's by making the time to read. We don't mean to sound condescending. We're just pointing out that it takes time to read, and you have to make the time to do it.

To make room in your schedule for reading, you have to treat it like a "big rock"—one of your top priorities. To do this, it's best to schedule the time you'll read beforehand, even if it's the night before. This way, when you wake up and review your daily calendar or to-do list, you'll have already scheduled time to read. When reading is in your calendar, you'll find ways to accomplish whatever else is on your list and be mentally prepared to read.

Let's take a quick look at regular times you can schedule to read.

Morning

Do you need to wake up fifteen or thirty minutes earlier to make time to read? Can you read while eating your breakfast or drinking your coffee or tea? What about listening to an audiobook while you're getting ready?

Personally, I (Jesse) don't really want to get up early, and my season of life with several young kids at home doesn't lend itself to a tremendous amount of self-care in the morning. Needless to say, my family and I are busy getting ready for the day. Jeff, on the other hand, reads off and on throughout the day, some of it scheduled and some during his downtime.

What's my point?

You don't have to squeeze reading into your morning routine. For some it works, and for others it doesn't. As you read the latest tips on maximizing your morning, take them with a grain of salt and find out what works best for you.

Commutes

Do you drive to work? Take a bus, subway, or train? These are great times you can listen to or read a book. According to one survey, the average one-way commute in the United States is 26.1 minutes, which totals nearly one hour per day.[8] This doesn't mean you have to listen to or read something the entire time. Consider spending just a portion of your commute with a book instead of listening to music or sports radio, or talking on the phone.

Breaks

Depending on your schedule, you'll take a break sometime during the day. If possible, leverage this time to relax with a book or learn something new. We understand this isn't possible for everyone at all times. But keep this in mind as you make reading a priority.

Lunch

At some time during your workday or shift, you'll eat lunch. This is a great time to score a few minutes of reading time. Plan ahead. Know what you're going to read. Find a spot to get away with your food, drink, and a book.

After Work

What are the top two or three things you do after work? Is it possible to replace something with reading? For me (Jesse), this doesn't work—at all. As soon as I'm done with work, it's family time with my wife and kids. But if you don't have regular obligations after work, reading a book can be a great way to unwind.

Before Bed

Your evening (or end of day) can be a gold mine for reading time. For many people, watching television or streaming a movie is the most common thing they do. Before you turn on a screen, press the pause button and pick up a book instead. Sit down or lie down with a book. Or turn on an audiobook to listen to before calling it a night.

Again, these are just a few key moments during the day when you can schedule reading into your calendar. What we shared here will give you some ideas. So use them as a starting place to make time to read that works for you.

Over to You

If you want to read more books, then you can. There's no secret, tip, or hack to reading other than picking up a book, cracking it open, and getting to work.

The biggest challenge you will face is with yourself. If you want to read more books, you will have to prioritize reading. There's no way around making this decision, and you're the only one who can make it. Thankfully, even though *you* are the biggest challenge you will face, *you* are also the answer to the problem in this situation.

Review the scientific benefits of reading. See how books can be the fuel to help you fulfill the vision of your life. Even if you have to wait for your feelings to catch up, lead yourself by committing to reading. Once you make this decision, the time you need to read will take care of itself.

Further Reading

Begin to tackle how to manage your time and energy and improve your ability to focus on what's most important in your life by reading:

Getting Things Done by David Allen

Essentialism: The Disciplined Pursuit of Less by Greg McKeown

Eat That Frog! by Brian Tracy

How to Build Your Reading Plan

A goal is not about what you accomplish.
It's about what you become.

Michael Hyatt

The first book I (Jesse) *remember* reading was in the summer of 2001.

I was twenty years old, and up until that point in my life I'd felt no interest in reading.

Apart from a few fleeting moments of academic interests, reading and education weren't a personal interest and weren't emphasized at home. Playing sports and having a fun time with friends were all that mattered.

But things changed for me that summer in two really big ways.

First, I had just met a girl (who is now my wife), and she liked to read. After our first conversation, I felt intimidated. She was intelligent, witty, and caught up with current events.

As for me, I was the proverbial collegiate meathead. I played football, and anything that whiffed of academics repulsed me.

Well, I wanted to see her again but knew I needed something intelligent to talk about the next time I saw her. So I visited a Waldenbooks store over the weekend, browsed the aisles, and bought a copy of *The Art of War* by Sun Tzu.

I can't recall why I picked up this specific book. But knowing who I was back then, I would wager it had something to do with the word *war* in the title.

After getting home, I sat down and read the entire book. While I found the writing archaic, clunky, and difficult to understand, my interest in impressing this new girl drove me to keep reading.

I can't say our second dinner date—at a Chili's in Charleston, West Virginia—paved the way for our marriage or that my love for books radically changed after reading *The Art of War*. But over the next few years, I did get married to her, and I slowly realized something else: I was reading a lot, which was an anomaly for me.

I'm not alone, either.

Rediscovering a Love for Reading

Apart from the textbooks I (Jeff) read in school, there's only one book I can honestly remember reading. It was J. R. R. Tolkien's *The Hobbit*.

The memory is still fresh. I was in the eighth grade, and *The Hobbit* was one book among several others I could choose from for an upcoming writing assignment. I don't recall the other options I was given. But upon diving into *The Hobbit*, I remember thinking I'd definitely made the right choice.

A lack of reading in my youth wasn't always the case. When I was in elementary school, I devoured books at home. I remember trips to the library with my mom and siblings. I have fond memories of her reading to the three of us from the Boxcar Children series or one of the many Dr. Seuss books. I was a big fan of the Hardy Boys and Encyclopedia Brown, and just about anything involving solving a mystery. In grade school, I was convinced I would grow up to be a detective. The books I read fed my imagination like nothing else. They made me believe I could do anything. But somewhere along the way, something changed. Reading all but disappeared from my homelife.

By the time I approached high school, I actually disliked reading. And not just *disliked* reading but disliked it with a passion. Between the assigned literature that didn't excite me and the mountains of homework on subjects I cared little about, I grew to dread anything involving reading. Reading a book felt like an unpleasant chore. It was something I *had* to do—not something I *got to* do.

Why share this with you?

If a love for reading can be reawakened in a guy like me or picked up by someone like Jesse, then there's hope for you too.

Get Ready to Read More Books

I haven't read a book in years. Reading is boring. Do you know how busy I am? Can't I just watch a video or listen to a podcast?

You may be thinking any of these things or others like them.

We get it.

Reading books isn't easy, it can feel like work, and taking a whiff of the vanilla notes from an old book may remind you of horrible experiences you had in school. These reasons and others may be enough for you to leave the books you own on your shelf collecting dust or on your wish list to purchase on some future date.

Don't let these excuses get in your way.

If you want to read more books, then hear us loud and clear: you can.

Over the past few years, between the two of us, we've read around 160 books per year. This includes books we've read or listened to for work, entertainment, and professional development and the chapter books I (Jesse) read to my kids.

Like you, we don't have a ton of spare time. As for me (Jesse), I have five kids, two cats, one dog, and a rabbit, I work full-time and wrote a book, and my family and I are involved in a church. As for Jeff, he's married, has dogs that could be mistaken for kids, runs a business and a podcast, teaches at a local university, and mentors budding entrepreneurs.

Regardless of your situation, you can read more books. But here's what you need to know: reading isn't something that happens by accident. You see, your time is limited. There are millions of books in circulation and thousands more being published weekly. It's impossible to read everything that has been or will be written. You have to choose wisely—especially if you want to benefit from what you read professionally.

To read more books, you need a reading plan. Thankfully, this isn't a complicated process. A reading plan is basically a checklist of books you want to read. So, instead of jumping from random book to random book, create a reading plan to help focus your efforts on what you should read to accomplish your goals.

Below is a process I use to determine what I'll read. For full disclosure, there are times I follow this plan religiously, and there are other times when I forget it even exists—plus there are seasons when I can't read as much as I'd like. But it's helped me to read more books, and I know it'll help you too.

MARK MILLER, VICE PRESIDENT OF HIGH-PERFORMANCE LEADERSHIP, CHICK-FIL-A, INC., AND INTERNATIONAL BESTSELLING AUTHOR OF *WIN EVERY DAY,* ON THE READING LIFE:

I learned from a mentor years ago that if you've got an hour to read, you should only read for thirty minutes. And you should spend the other thirty minutes trying to figure out: What does it mean and what will you do?

If you take that to heart, you might say, "Well, that reduces my reading time." But I would say it probably has a huge impact on your effectiveness. I'm trying to be sure that I still have enough margin that I build in my life, in my calendar, to actually think about what I'm reading.

We (family) moved not too long ago and I've got more "car time," so I'm doing more Audible (audiobook app). I probably don't retain as much as I would if I sat down with a book, but if I can get 60 or 70 percent, compared to 80 or 90 percent, to me that's better than nothing. What I'll (often) do is I'll listen to it and then buy a (physical) copy. I'm almost using Audible for screening books.

Again, time to think, to assess, to reflect—I think that's how you internalize it so that you can actually act on it.

Step 1: Know Your Why

Why do you want to read more books?

Do you want to learn a new skill? Are you conducting research for a new project? Are you interested in reading a captivating story?

As we shared in chapter 2, there are many benefits to reading more books. But for the sake of making your reading plan, it's essential to clarify your "why" before moving forward. This will not only help you build your reading plan but will help you push through, change your habits, and read more books—even when you feel like quitting.

So, why do you want to read more books? Do you want to learn new skills? Do you need help overcoming a challenge? Are you interested in expanding your vocabulary, learning about a certain historical era or current events, or becoming a better conversationalist? Whatever your motivation, now is the time to tap into it. Your why will fuel your progress toward accomplishing your reading goals.

For me (Jesse), I read books to help me professionally; to gain new insights as a husband, parent, and friend; to learn about history, current events, and influential people; and to explore personal interests and seek entertainment.

Action step: identify one to five reasons why you want to read more books.

Step 2: Set Realistic Reading Goals

How many books should you read this month or year?

Well, it depends.

There are multiple variables that go into this equation. How many books you can read will be different from someone else. So be careful not to imitate the reading habits of another person who has been reading for years or is in a different stage of life.

The best thing to do is compare how much you read today with yesterday. You might be ready to read one book per month, and that's okay. Or you might be prepared to read one book per week. Regardless of your situation, it's best to set a realistic goal for yourself.

For starters, read chapter 6 to think through how much time you can devote to reading. You won't be able to read fifty books this year if you only have the time to devote to reading twelve. What's more, if you know you're about to enter a busy season of life—such as increased responsibilities at home or work, travel, or holidays—keep that in consideration. You will only have so much time you can devote to reading, and there are times when your reading time will be occupied by something else, and that's okay. Creating a reading plan and habit is more about maintaining a long-term commitment, not fulfilling short-term goals.

Talking about realistic goals, don't plan on reading a hundred books this year if you haven't read a book in a while. You have to learn to crawl before you can walk—let alone run a marathon of reading. Instead, make a plan for how many books you will read in the next three months.

It doesn't matter how you schedule your reading time, such as "I'll read fifteen minutes per day" or "I'll read three hundred pages per week." The biggest idea we want you to take away from this step is that you're making the time you need in your schedule for reading. This way you can get a better idea of what you're capable of doing. Set yourself up to succeed rather than crash and burn in a fire of disappointment.

Action step: determine how many books you want to read in the next month, quarter, or year. Now, revisit chapter 6 to figure out how to make the time in your schedule to accomplish your reading goal.

Step 3: Pick Categories or Genres

You probably have some books in mind you want to read. But before you finalize your choices, think through the types of books you want to read in broad categories.

Identifying these categories will help you select specific books to fulfill your goals and ensure you maintain a well-balanced reading diet, and it makes it easier to plan and organize what you're going to read.

At the moment, I (Jesse) have six categories I focus on: business, history, theology, culture, children's, and fiction. I decided on these categories based on the goals I identified above.

For example, for my business category, I'll regularly read books on marketing, management, and entrepreneurship. With this category, I'm constantly reading books that help sharpen me professionally. The children's category contains the books I read out loud to my kids. This includes some fun books and short titles, but mostly it involves classic books.

The other categories I've identified are areas of personal interest. Though I'm not necessarily a huge fan of fiction, reading in this category helps stretch me as a reader and learn storytelling from some of the best writers.

When it comes to naming the categories you want to read, identify what types of books will help you accomplish your goals and what you actually enjoy reading. What types of books will most influence your life, work, hobbies, and aspirations? What types of books do you like to read for their entertainment value?

If you need help with parenting, plan on reading a few parenting books. If you're looking for new business ideas, pick up some titles on entrepreneurship. If you're planning on starting a garden this year, then read a few region-specific gardening books to help you get off to a good start.

Here is a short list of different genres for you to consider:

religion

mystery

business

travel

history

science

comics

biography

fantasy

children's literature

Now, categorizing your reading isn't necessary for every season of your life. There were times in my past when I had to focus on only one or two categories because I was trying to learn a new skill or conduct research for a new project, like writing a book.

Action step: pick three or more categories or genres that will help you reach your goal, or one or two categories that will help you learn something new.

Step 4: Track Your Reading

Keeping track of your reading plan is like creating a map: it'll help you reach your destination. To track your reading, you can simply create a checklist with a pen and paper, use a notetaking app, or create a spreadsheet. It doesn't matter how you track your reading, as long as you use a manageable system.

If you're following this process, all you need to do is create three columns. Label the first column *category*. This is the column you'll use to track what genre or category you choose. Label the second column *title*, which is where you'll place the title of your book. Finally, label the third column *author*, which is where you can track the author's name. If you want, you can add more columns to track whatever else you'd like, such as how you rate the book, or perhaps to have a place to record your notes and thoughts.

Regardless of what system you use to track your reading, the goal is not necessarily to fill out the entire calendar but to know what you're reading this month and the next so you can be prepared and have what you need to read. This way you're not waiting around or spending time gathering material when you could be reading.

My calendar is currently filled out for the next three months, and I have a laundry list of books identified that I want to read. But my list regularly changes.

Reading is a fluid activity. If you're not enjoying a book or you've already grasped what the author is trying to say in the

Download a copy of this reading plan spreadsheet at www.readtoleadbook.com.

first fifty pages, feel free to abandon it. There's no reason to plod through a book if you don't want to or have to.

Action step: create a tracker (reading log) for your reading plan.

Step 5: Choose Your Titles

Here comes the fun part.

You have a reading goal. You've made a plan. You know what categories you're going to read. Now you get to pick the individual books.

Don't get bogged down by choosing books. Ideally, it's best to identify enough books to read for the next two or three months to help you fulfill your reading goal. But at the end of the day, you just have to know what you're going to read next.

To complete this step, revisit chapter 5 and work through the provided questions to identify books you'd like to read. As you do so, choose books you're going to read based on the categories or genres you selected in step three above.

You can also ask your friends, scan bestseller lists or Goodreads, read classics, or explore titles similar to your favorite books.

Now, these book choices are not set in stone. Feel free to rearrange the individual titles you want to read. Your goal with this step is to identify what books you want to read. If you receive a great recommendation or feel you can't handle one more business book, then take a break. Read something else.

Action step: revisit the list of books you created from chapter 5 and make a list of three to five titles you want to read for every category you chose above.

Over to You _____

What books should you read?

How many books do you want to read?

How much time can you devote to reading?

Now create a reading plan to tie this all together. That's what this chapter—and section—is all about: helping you to clarify your reading goals, create margin in your life, and develop a reading plan to read more books.

In the next section and following chapters, we're going to build on this foundation. We're going to share with you hard-fought reading advice to help you read faster and to comprehend and retain more of what you read, and we'll also share other tips you can use to maximize what you read, learn new skills, and boost your career.

Further Reading _____

Consume *The 7 Habits of Highly Effective People* by Stephen Covey to develop a principle-centered approach to your life, career, and reading plan.

THE SMARTER WAY TO READ BOOKS

CHAPTER 8

How to Absorb a Book into Your Bloodstream

The reading of all good books is like a conversation with the finest minds of the past centuries.

Descartes

Who is someone you admire from a distance?

Someone you'd like to ask a question?

There are several people who immediately come to mind when I (Jesse) think about this answer: Theodore Roosevelt, Ryan Holiday, and Francis Schaeffer. Two of these three people have passed away, but I can still enjoy a conversation with them, as well as Ryan Holiday, without knowing them personally. How? By reading their books.

You see, reading a book is like having a conversation with the author.

If you're reading a nonfiction book, then you're most likely interested in learning from the author. Whether you are looking for an answer to a question, a solution to a problem, or how to do something new, you purchased their book to help you along the way.

This sounds obvious, but it's important to point out.

When you purchase a nonfiction book (like the one you're reading now), you do so because you believe the author knows more about the topic than you do. If this isn't the case, then let us offer you some unsolicited advice: don't buy their book.

To really get everything out of the books you read—to absorb the material into your bloodstream—you need to think of yourself as a student while you read. You want to treat the book in front of you as if you are sitting in a classroom with the author.

You are the student.

The author is the teacher.

And this shift in mindset makes all the difference.

We can't know if you consider yourself a good student or not. But you can be an excellent student of whatever book you're reading without any formal training, literary background, or off-the-chart IQ. It really boils down to choosing to be an *active* rather than a *passive* reader. As you read, you can choose to haphazardly skim a book, not take any notes, and read without actually thinking about what you're reading. Or you can choose to focus on what you read, ask questions along the way for clarification, and prepare yourself to apply the lessons you learn afterward. The choice is yours.

There are times when you will read for leisure or entertainment, but for the purpose of this chapter, we are talking about reading for the sake of learning.

Before getting into the nitty-gritty, let's take a moment to talk about reading comprehension and retention. We're not going to get too technical, but there's a difference between the two you need to know, because they influence how you approach the books you read.

Reading Comprehension versus Reading Retention

What's the difference between reading comprehension and reading retention? The former is understanding what you read as you read, whereas the latter is later remembering what you read. Can you understand the books you read? This is comprehension. Do you remember the book or recall specific details? This is retention.

Don't treat this difference too lightly.

Reading comprehension and reading retention are two different skills that require two different approaches. By

EDWARD THOMAS, SENIOR ENLISTED LEADER OF OPERATIONS AND INTERNATIONAL LAW, UNITED STATES DEPARTMENT OF THE AIR FORCE, ON THE READING LIFE:

While reading a book (digital or hard copy), I enjoy the ability to make highlights or bookmark a page to refer back to at a later point for deeper thought. Last year I crossed the mental hurdle to also start listening to audiobooks (listening to podcasts helped me make the jump). As information in the book is presented that interests me or I want to learn more about, in the app I use to listen to the book, I (digitally) bookmark the time and continue to do so until the book is complete. At that point I go back, relisten to the bookmarks, and create a tab in my Microsoft OneNote to gather my thoughts on the topics. That is when I am able to further think through the material and find ways to apply the information.

learning these two skills, you'll be well on your way to absorbing what you read. In the rest of this chapter, we're going to show you how to master both.

A Step-by-Step Guide to Absorbing a Book

To absorb a book into your bloodstream, there are six steps you need to take. This process should be done in its entirety and in the order below for you to best digest the material you read.

Step 1: Get an Overview

Before reading a book, fight the urge to sit down, open it, and start reading from beginning to end. Stop! It's best to take a few moments to preview what you are about to read. This way you can prepare to comprehend as much as possible.

This may sound counterintuitive, but hear us out.

Over the years, different reading comprehension methods (SQR3 and PQRST, for example) have included this step for one reason: it works. Giving yourself a preview of what you are about to read goes a long way in preparing you to become an active reader, which ultimately enhances your reading comprehension.

When it comes to getting an overview, here's what you need to do:

- Know what you are going to read (e.g., one chapter).
- Skim the introduction and conclusion.
- Familiarize yourself with the chapter titles and section headings.
- Identify any points of emphasis (e.g., text in bold or italic).
- Limit yourself to three to five minutes total.

Remember, the point of this step isn't to learn everything. The idea is to get ready to ask questions and engage on a deeper level with the material, which leads us to the next step.

Step 2: Ask Questions

Reading a book is a conversation.[1] And at the heart of any good conversation are some well-thought-out questions.

As a reader, you don't want to ask just any question. This isn't the time for small talk or locker-room chatter. You want to ask the right questions in the right order. This way you'll understand what the author intended to say, not what you thought he or she said, and there's a big difference between the two.

Think about it like this. Imagine you are standing face-to-face with an author to discuss his or her book. This book has the potential to help you solve a problem, answer a question, or overcome a challenge you're facing. To maximize your time and learn as much as you possibly can, it's essential to prepare yourself for this chat. And the way you do this is by asking good questions.

Knowing what questions to ask before reading is one simple way to boost your comprehension. Preparing a set of questions ahead of time will activate your mind to find the answers in what you're reading. In a sense, they will be the compass guiding your efforts.

In boosting your reading comprehension, here are three questions you can use:

- What question is this chapter trying to answer?
- What problem does this chapter want to solve?
- What questions would I like answered in this chapter?

Here's one popular trick you can use too: adapt the chapter titles and subheadings into questions. For example, in chapter 10 of this book, one of the subheadings reads "One Must-Know Tip before Skim-Reading." To convert this into a question, you could ask "What is one must-know tip before skim-reading?"

We understand you probably learned these or similar reading comprehension tips in elementary school. But we also know it's a good idea to have a refresher.

Most of the time, these questions will be enough to boost your reading comprehension. But there are other times when you'll want to take a deeper dive into the material you're reading. To accomplish this higher level of reading, let's turn to the masters of reading books well—Mortimer Adler and Charles Van Doren.

In *How to Read a Book: The Classic Guide to Intelligent Reading*, these authors suggest answering the following four questions in the order they're presented to mine the depths of whatever book you're reading.

1. What Is the Book about as a Whole?

To get the answer to this question, you'll have to read the entire book. Afterward, the authors suggest identifying the main theme and then identifying how it is developed throughout the book.

At this point, your goal is to ensure you have crystalized the main idea. In the next step, it's time to get into the finer details.

2. What Is Being Said in Detail, and How?

In answering this question, you're digging into a book to uncover how the author is supporting the main theme. One of the best ways to do this is to write a summary of the book. From creating an outline of every chapter that highlights the main point and supporting points to summarizing your key insights from the book, there's no one-size-fits-all approach to summarizing a book.

Regardless of how you approach the answer to this question, the main thing is to take this step and analyze a book. How you technically do this can be debated. The good thing is that this step will take your understanding of the book to a new level.

3. Is the Book True, in Whole or in Part?

All right, so an author wrote a book on a topic and made multiple supporting points along the way. Is what they are saying true? Did they prove their point? Or are there weaknesses in their argument?

Before you try to answer whether or not the book is true, we want to share one word of caution: be sure to answer the first two questions in this process before spending time here. If you do not know what an author said, there's no way you can actually agree or disagree with him or her.

4. What of It?

At first, this question may sound tongue-in-cheek. But this is where the rubber meets the road in examining a book.

In the end, you've read a book, and now is the time to know why the author thought it was essential to write it and whether or not that's important to you. For example, did their book answer your questions? Can you now solve your problem? Do you need to seek out additional resources?

Depending upon your reading needs, you may or may not have to go through this entire process laid out by Adler and

Van Doren. Answering these four questions may be more suited for times when you have to know a book inside and out—such as for an exam or school assignment. For what it's worth, we don't follow through with these four questions every time we read a book.

You're now ready to have a conversation with the author. You've previewed their book and you're ready to ask questions. It's time to get ready to capture your answers, which leads us to the next step.

Step 3: Write in Your Book

Personally, I (Jesse) am a fan of physical books. My family and I own well over two thousand books and probably just a few dozen e-books.

I like the way physical books feel in my hands. How they smell. But most importantly of all, reading a physical book is ideal for my reading style and places me in the best position to have a conversation with the author.

Writing in your book is a great way to answer the questions we just talked about.[2] I guess you can take notes in your e-reader. But that's not for me.

One caveat: jotting down fancy symbols or highlighting everything you read doesn't necessarily help you retain information.[3] But that's not the point anyway. Asking questions, actively engaging with the material, and highlighting and writing in your book along the way will position you to better comprehend what you're reading. In one way, you can say writing in your book is like talking with the author.

Here's what we mean.

It would be awkward if you met an author in person and just sat there while they spoke the entire time. It's challenging to keep a conversation going when there's only one person talking, and it'd be hard for you to retain what they're saying without taking notes. If you were meeting with an author in person, and you knew they had the answers to your questions, we bet you would have a pen and paper (or phone) ready to take notes. This is like writing in your book.

Here are a dozen ways you can liberally write in your book:

1. Underline or highlight interesting sentences.
2. Make vertical lines in the margins for interesting paragraphs or sections.
3. Write questions or comments in the margins.
4. Answer the questions previously mentioned in the margins.
5. Circle key words or points.
6. Use a dot or asterisk to capture a main idea.
7. Write notes in the margins.
8. Write down the page number where an idea is repeated.
9. Write numbers beside a sequence of points.
10. Summarize each chapter on the blank page between chapters.
11. Create an outline of the book on blank pages in the book.
12. Summarize the main idea of the book on the blank pages at the back.

Don't be afraid to write in your book. For us, it'd be an honor if you took notes and made comments within these pages as you read this book. Make marks. Highlight sentences.

Fold down the top corners of pages (called dog-ears). Jot down notes. Leave your thoughts in the margins. Converse with the book you're reading.

Not convinced you should write in your book? Reading a library book? No sweat. Feel free to use sticky notes to mark places in your book. If you go this route, consider purchasing a set of multicolor flags you can use to capture different ideas. For example, you can use a blue flag to draw your attention to a quote and a pink flag to remind you of an essential point.

Writing in your book (or using flags) activates your mind, helps you to comprehend what you read, and is a great way to keep track of your ideas, which takes us to our next step.

Step 4: Take Notes

After taking the first three steps, you'll know the book. But as we mentioned earlier, comprehending what you read is different than retaining what you read. In the next few steps, we'll walk you through four ways you can better retrieve your insights.

When reading and highlighting what you read, it's essential to capture these key findings in notes. As with many things in life, there are several equally valuable ways you can take notes.

What works well for us or someone else may not be a good fit for you, and that's okay. Use what we share here as a starting point.

Keep Notes in Your Books

In the previous step, we suggested keeping notes in your books. Whether you summarize chapters, mention highlights, or rewrite key insights in the book, using the book itself as a notepad is one way to keep your thoughts in one spot.

This is my (Jeff's) favorite method for notetaking. Almost every book has one or more blank pages near the beginning and also toward the end. The way I keep notes in my books is by creating an index on these blank pages.

When I come across a phrase or concept I want to remember, or something that sparked an idea, I write down the page number in my index and add a brief one-line note about why it matters.

One of the reasons I love this method so much (thank you, Jonathan Milligan, for sharing it with me) is because I never have to remember where my notes are. They're in the book itself, and I can refer back to them with ease. Talk about a win.

Use Notecards

This is the method I (Jesse) recently started using. As I read a book, I make marks similar to the suggestions we shared above. Afterward, I'll go back through the book page by page looking for my marks, and then I'll write down quotes or key insights on index cards. I started doing this after hearing about it from Ryan Holiday.

On each of these index cards, I'll also write down a theme on the top righthand corner, such as "marketing," "religion," or "life," so I can easily sort them into categories. Next, I'll write down a note, insight, or quote and include its page number so I can find the reference later. Lastly, I'll store the cards in my "commonplace book," which is a fancy way of saying my index card file.

I held off on doing this for years, and to be honest, I regret that I waited so long. It has increased my retention, and my index card file makes it easy to store and retrieve notes later.

Use a Word Processor or Notetaking App

For many people, a word processor like Microsoft Word or Google Docs or a notetaking app such as Evernote or Apple Notes is where they store their notes. This is what I (Jesse) kind of did for a while.

Obviously you can keep your notes in one of these pieces of software, and I have to admit, it's a whole lot easier to store your outlines and lengthy summaries this way.

Regardless of which option you choose, pick one, commit to it, and don't get too hung up on your process. In time, you'll figure out what notetaking method works best for you. Even though this step is geared toward increasing your retention, it's also helpful in further solidifying your comprehension, since you're reengaging with the book.

Use a Notebook

Another technique I (Jeff) lean on the most for my reading notes is a single notebook. I don't use this notebook for anything other than keeping notes from what I've read. This notebook is always by my side while I'm reading. I add to it regularly, and only once it's full do I move on to a new notebook.

There's one drawback I've discovered: after filling up multiple notebooks, it can be difficult to find which one contains the notes for a particular book I want to revisit. At first I was literally opening them up one at a time and leafing through them. But one way I make this easier now is by inserting a new sticky note divider in my notebook whenever I start a new book. I generally write an abbreviated version of the book's title on the divider so I can easily see it on the portion of the note that protrudes from the notebook. This makes it easy to scan the notebook for the book notes I'm looking for.

Step 5: Review Your Notes

Here's the thing about notes: they're not helpful if you never look at them.

How often you review your notes is up to you and your situation. If you're a student preparing for an exam, it's ideal to keep what you study fresh by frequently reviewing it. For simply retaining what you read, consider revisiting the notes you've written every several months or more.

To be successful in this step, it's key to nail down the previous step. For example, in preparing to write this book, I (Jesse) skimmed back through a dozen or more books to help me wrap my brain around what I wanted to share. Even though this was prior to my time of using a notecard system, I still had left marks in the books I read, which made it easy for me to write down the essential ideas.

Reviewing your notes is not only helpful for writing books but for many things. From preparing for a presentation to developing new business ideas to drafting a speech, it will be like adding nitroglycerin to your fuel tank: it'll add more power to your work.

Step 6: Take Action

There's one thing a book cannot do for you. Know what it is?

It cannot make you do anything—only you can do that.

You may have found the answer to your problem in a book. But if you don't actually do something about it, then you're still stuck. It's not like the author can hold your hand and make you do what they are suggesting.

You see, "a practical problem can only be solved by action itself."[4]

The words you read cannot stay within the confines of your mind. You have to actively wrestle with what you're reading by asking questions, engaging with the content, and applying it to your life. Not applying what you read is easy to do. You read a book on healthy living, finances, business, or whatever, and instead of applying the lessons you learned you just move on to the next book.

We're not saying you need to reflect upon every book you read for weeks, months, or years. But we are saying that if you have a particular problem you're trying to resolve, then at some point in time you have to actually implement what you're learning. This is a simple concept. But it's difficult in practice.

What did you learn from the book you're reading? Think about the top one to three lessons that will provide the best results for your situation and apply them to your life. Set a goal. Share that goal with someone else. See what results you gain from taking action on what you read.

Over to You

Reading is fun, entertaining, and a wonderful leisurely activity. But if you want to learn from the books you read, then you must be ready to have a conversation with the author. You'll need to be ready to ask questions, review your notes, and take action on what you read. This shift in the way you approach reading will help you solve your problems and overcome the obstacles you face.

Now that you know how to absorb a book into your bloodstream, let's talk next about how you can increase your reading speed, read more books, and learn more than you thought possible.

Further Reading

We owe much of what we learned about reading comprehension and retention to Mortimer Adler and Charles Van Doren's classic book, *How to Read a Book: The Classic Guide to Intelligent Reading.*

CHAPTER 9

Double (or Triple) Your Reading Speed in Minutes

With ordinary talent and extraordinary
perseverance, all things are attainable.

Thomas Fowell Buxton

The most profitable sixty minutes of professional development I (Jesse) have ever spent was in 2005. I'd just started
graduate school, and the school offered a speed-reading
course. Since I'd missed the course during the day, the instructor was kind enough to meet with me one-on-one and
go over the lessons, which took about an hour.

This small investment of time and the grace extended by
my instructor were game-changers. The lessons he shared—
which are similar to what you'll find in this book—revolu-
tionized my ability to read, study, and learn. They helped
me to conduct extensive research for assignments, keep up
with the demands of school while working and starting my
family, and position myself to learn skills and gain insight
for new jobs and opportunities.

Learning plays an essential part in your professional development. Of course, this includes learning from life, school, and your experiences. But it also includes what you learn and apply from books.

Let's park here for one moment.

If you could increase your reading speed, think about how many more books you could read, how much time you would save, and how many more ideas and concepts you could explore. Could this help you advance in your career, learn new skills, or both?

We think so.

But let's be honest: trying to read more books can be frustrating.

There's work, family, and big books. If you're feeling overwhelmed, you're not alone. Like many people, you have a list the length of your arm of books you want to read.

Thankfully, you don't have to be like John Travolta's character in *Phenomenon*, George Malley, who could read two to three books per day after apparently being struck by a flash of light from heaven that brought him superintelligence. Reading faster is more about learning good reading habits than about being born with special gifts or being struck by lightning.

In this chapter, we're going to explore practical ways you can double or perhaps even triple your reading speed. But before we can get into the details, we have to talk about some common misconceptions associated with reading faster.

Is "Speed-Reading" a Farce?

Many misconceptions surround speed-reading—and rightfully so. From outlandish claims to simple misunderstandings, the water is a bit murky. Let's take a closer look at some mischaracterizations you may have.

"Speed-Reading Doesn't Work."

Well, it depends.

If you're addressing claims of being able to read thousands of words per minute with crystal clear comprehension and retention, then sure, we'd agree with you. And so does the scientific community. Study after study reveals that it's a Herculean task to read more than six hundred words per minute (wpm) without losing serious comprehension.

Now, if you're talking about increasing your reading speed until you are faster than the average college student or adult, then hang on a second. That's what we're talking about.

Remember, the average adult reads 238 wpm when it comes to nonfiction books and 260 wpm while reading fiction. If this is your reading speed, you're in luck. After you unlearn bad reading habits, create a few good reading habits, and apply a few tips, you'll be well on your way to doubling or tripling your reading speed. But if you're already at an above-average rate, say 350–450 wpm, you can still increase your reading speed, but it won't be as significant.

What's the moral of the story?

Speed-reading works. It just depends on what type of speed-reading you're talking about.

"Slow Readers Comprehend More."

Not exactly.

From bad reading habits to learning disabilities, there are several reasons why you may not read as fast as you'd like or can. Know what else? Reading slowly doesn't actually mean you're able to comprehend more. As far as we can tell, there's no scientific evidence to back up this claim. If anything, studies show rereading the same material or reading everything word-for-word doesn't mean you'll comprehend more than someone who can read faster or knows how to scan books well.

"Reading Faster Leads to Less Comprehension."

Yeah, that dog won't hunt.

When you learn good reading habits, your reading comprehension will improve too. Even when you use the speed-reading techniques from chapters 9 and 10, your ability to understand what you read will improve because you'll also learn ways to grasp what you're reading.

Remember, slow readers are not necessarily the best readers when it comes to comprehension. Focus less on how fast you should or shouldn't read and strive to read well at a comfortable pace for you.

With these reading misconceptions out of the way, we'll get ready to help you increase your reading speed. But first, you'll need to figure out how fast you read.

How to Determine Your Reading Speed

To make any forward progress, you have to start from somewhere.

When it comes to increasing your reading speed, you have to know how fast you can read. Without this baseline knowledge, you won't be able to make significant progress.

Before we help you figure out your reading speed, let us remind you not to get fixated on how fast you read compared to someone else. It's always best to compare your reading speed today with how fast you read yesterday. The average reading speeds for adults just mentioned (238 wpm for non-fiction, 260 for fiction) may encourage or discourage you. But hang tight. Help is on the way.

At this point it's natural to wonder how fast you can read. Thankfully, you can figure it out in only a few minutes. Here are the four steps you need to take to test how many words per minute (wpm) you can read.

Step 1: Get Your Reading Material

For this test, you want to pick reading material you *normally* read. This can be something from a magazine, book (nonfiction or fiction), blog post, newspaper, or whatever. The goal is to stick with something you usually read. This way your test can be as accurate as possible.

If you normally read the *Wall Street Journal*, then you don't want to test your reading speed with *Curious George*. Likewise, you want to avoid using a dictionary or material with small fonts and margins or a lot of pictures and graphs.

Step 2: Set a Timer and Mark Your Starting Point

For this exercise, you're going to read for one minute. Before you start, set a timer for one minute. It doesn't matter what kind of timer you use as long as you're ready to time yourself.

Before you begin, don't forget to mark your starting point.

Step 3: Read for One Minute and Mark Your Stopping Place

All right, now it's time to read. Start your timer and read until the time expires. As you read, keep these three tips in mind: (1) Don't look at the time as you read, (2) Don't try to read faster than normal, and (3) Just read at your average pace. Following these three guidelines will keep you from throwing off your results.

Now, don't forget to mark wherever you stopped reading.

Step 4: Stop and Count

It's time to get your results.

One way you can do this is to count every word from your starting point to your stopping place.

Another way to find your reading speed is to take an average. Here's how:

1. Count the number of words per line for four lines of text.
2. Divide this number by four.
3. Count the number of lines you read in your test.
4. Multiply the number from step 2 by the number from step 3 to get your average reading speed.

For example, for this reading test, let's say whatever you chose to read had a total of forty-four words in the first four lines of text. And let's say you read forty-two lines in one minute. Here's what your results would be:

$$44 \div 4 = 11$$
$$11 \times 42 = 462 \text{ wpm}$$

From this example, your reading speed would be 462 wpm. When gauging your reading speed, it's best to take this test three to five times and average your results together. This will give you a good idea about how fast you can read.

Not happy with your speed?

Don't worry if your reading speed doesn't compare well to the averages above or how fast you wish you could read today. Learning how to read faster isn't about where you start. It's about where you're going. And you can increase your reading speed at any age.

How to Double (or Triple) Your Reading Speed

Now it's time to learn how you can potentially increase your reading speed.

1. Prepare Your Reading Environment

Your reading environment will influence how well you can read. Trying to read in a "bad" environment is like trying to walk up a down escalator—you'll go nowhere fast, and you'll likely stumble and fall along the way. A bad environment can include a number of things, including bad

ANDREW CHROSTOWSKI, CEO AT REALWEAR INC., ON THE READING LIFE:

As a child, books were my imagination factory and time machine. I couldn't talk with Socrates, but I could read what Plato related about him. . . . I could go 20,000 leagues under the sea thanks to Jules Verne. Both drove a lifelong interest in history and science. My uncle, who had a PhD in history, taught me to read for self-learning, how to speed-read, and how to remember and use what I read. My study of self-improvement, leadership, and business were all driven by books and purposeful reading.

seating, poor lighting, and distractions. Distractions come in all shapes and sizes. For Jesse, distractions (albeit good at times) often come in the form of five kids, one dog, two cats, one rabbit, email, social media, push notifications, and a flood of instant messages. For Jeff, there aren't any children running about but instead three dogs who think they need constant attention. Seriously though, for both of us (and probably you), it's really the notifications from emails, social media, and so on that can be the problem. If Jeff wants to read with complete focus, it's necessary for him to don his noise-canceling headphones.

Having a place you can concentrate is essential to reading well.

The ideal reading environment will differ from person to person. But, in general, you want to find a place where you can both concentrate and be comfortable. This can be somewhere in your home, outside, or, for you anomalies, a coffee shop.

What is more, consider listening to music to drown out other noise and help you focus on what you're reading. Several studies suggest that listening to certain types of music can help you concentrate.[1] While Jesse doesn't find listening to any kind of music helpful, Jeff prefers to use his noise-canceling headphones to listen to some ambient music (i.e., instrumental only, and absolutely nothing recognizable or with lyrics).

What's the big idea? Know what does and doesn't help you to focus, and create a reading environment that lends itself to boosting your concentration.

2. Read in Short Blocks of Time

Even though your brain isn't technically a muscle, you should treat it like one when reading. Just like your body will become physically exhausted from exercise, so too will your brain become mentally exhausted from reading. This is why you should read in short blocks of time.

We prefer to read in twenty-minute blocks. We don't set a timer when doing this. But it's a general principle we follow, and it works for us. You may be able to read for longer stretches of time, or you may need to consider starting with a shorter block of time, say five to ten minutes.

Whatever timeframe you land on, keep this in mind: several different studies have found that it's best to read in short bursts at high speeds in order to maintain your reading comprehension.[2] Read. Push your limits. And see what size block of reading time works for you.

3. Guide Your Reading

When you were taught how to read, there's a good chance it began as reading word-for-word aloud. "Hot." "Cat." "Red." "Ball." As you progressed in your ability to read, you then transitioned to reading to yourself, and this is what's called subvocalization. This is a good thing, but it can reduce your reading speed. Here's why: your reading speed can be faster than your talking speed.

Before you get ahead of yourself, we're not promoting or promising the ability to eliminate your internal speech (subvocalization). Many studies show this isn't possible, and that's okay. We're simply suggesting you can read faster than you talk.

To increase your reading speed, you don't have to read every word. Reading is more about understanding the ideas behind the words and their context than the words themselves. To a degree, you're already doing this. For example, when you see a stop sign, an LOL, or an exhibit dated 150

BC, you don't read the signs or letters. This works because you know the idea behind the abbreviations and symbols.

To limit your subvocalization and lead yourself to read phrases and capture ideas, there's one common way to improve your reading speed, and that's by guiding your reading. Said another way, you are simply using your hand or finger, pen or pencil, or whatever else you choose as a pointer to guide yourself as you read.

With your pointer in hand, place it beneath the first word you're going to read. Now sweep your pointer across the page from left to right at a pace that forces you to read faster while maintaining comprehension (remember, be ready to mark your book as you read). This reading method will help you to focus, read phrases instead of words, and continually progress instead of rereading and pausing after every line.

At first, this method of reading will be uncomfortable. But this idea is essential to improving your reading speed, and the next method below builds on it. Before moving on, set aside ten to fifteen minutes to practice guiding. Choose the kind of reading material you normally read. This way you can compare your results from reading with this method to your previous reading speed.

4. The Hop Method

The hop method builds on the guiding method above. But unlike the guiding method, where you're moving your pointer in one continuous motion, with the hop method you'll use your pointer to touch beneath the text you are reading about one-third and again about two-thirds down the line. As you hop along, follow your pointer. The first hop (touch) will lead you to see the first several words, and the second hop (touch) will lead you to take in the remainder of the line.

For practicing this technique, consider starting out with three to five hops per line, and then move to two hops if you can. If the lines of the text you're reading are long, then you may need to use three to five hops or more to take in all of the material.

As a reminder, pace your hops in a way that challenges you to read faster. But you don't want to move at a pace that's impossible for you to maintain or to comprehend what you're reading. As you push yourself to read faster, you'll rely less on subvocalization and reading every word (fixation).

Over to You

At the end of the day, there's one primary way you can improve your reading, and that's by reading more books. Learning how to read faster is equal parts learning how to read well and reading more. As you read, you'll build a more robust vocabulary, better understand the structure of writing, and transform into a faster—and better—reader. There's no more effective way to read faster and better than by doing the work itself: reading.

Further Reading

Increasing your reading speed will take focus and discipline, and these two books provide pertinent advice:

Deep Work: Rules for Focused Success in a Distracted World by Cal Newport
The ONE Thing: The Surprisingly Simple Truth behind Extraordinary Results by Gary Keller and Jay Papasan

CHAPTER 10

How to "Read" a 220-Page Book in One Hour

There is no deficit in human resources;
the deficit is in human will.

Martin Luther King Jr.

Staying competitive is challenging. Whether you're competing for a new job or running a business, staying ahead and staying relevant often requires learning something new. Even after mastering the techniques we share in this book, you may still feel like you're behind the eight ball and unable to get ahead with all of the books you'd like to read. But don't stress yourself out. There's a way you can read a book in one hour.

Well, let us rephrase that: you can *skim* a book in one hour and *comprehend* the most essential information you need to know.

This isn't a magic trick or snake oil we're peddling. There's a way you can skim a book—fast—and discover the big takeaways you need to know.

Before we show you how, we'd like to point out this is more than an opinion; science is on our side.

Skimming a Book Is Not Only for Slackers, Says Science

Skimming a book isn't only for those of us who forgot to read something or just need to cram in a few pages because we didn't plan properly. Far from it. Studies show that skim-reading has a couple of scientific benefits when it comes to reading a large swath of material and comprehending what we read.

In one way, skim-reading is like learning where you're going ahead of time before taking a long trip. Skimming gives you the lay of the land so you know what to expect, which naturally makes it easier for you to get to where you're going. According to one study, sophomore university students who skimmed their assigned reading first accelerated their normal rate of reading in most cases.[1] It's like our example about a road trip. When you're comfortable with your directions (or know what you're going to read), you're able to get to your final destination faster.

In another study, researchers discovered that skim-readers were better able to grasp the main points of the text they were reading compared to those who were "normal readers."[2] What is more, when it came to understanding the less important, secondary information, there was no difference in performance between the groups.

Finally, in a different study, researchers found that trained speed-readers possess an advantage in their reading speed and comprehension versus nontrained speed-readers.[3] In other words, practiced speed-readers better understood how to skim-read and pull out the essential concepts.

This means you can learn how to quickly skim large amounts of material fast while maintaining comprehension.

Skim-reading is more than haphazardly skipping around the pages of your book. There's an actual science and art to doing it well. So, let's get into learning the details.

But first, there's a time and place for skim-reading.

When You Should Not Read This Way

Not every tool can accomplish every job. It's not like you can use a hammer to mow your grass or a table saw to hang up a picture in your living room. In the same way, speed-reading techniques are not suitable for every occasion.

Here are three times when you don't want to skim-read.

1. Reading Something Unfamiliar

Do you need to learn something new? Is there a book or article you have to read, and you're not familiar with the topic? Then don't think about skim-reading.

One big part of being able to read faster is possessing an understanding of the material. If you need to learn something new for school or work, or you're diving into something new you want to learn, then prepare to go slower than usual at first. You can't rush learning new vocabulary and concepts.

2. Reading for Pleasure

Call us crazy, but you can read for fun. Everything you read doesn't have to be another task to accomplish. You can pick up classic literature, a mystery novel, something from a bestseller list, or whatever suits your fancy to read for entertainment.

When reading for pleasure, relax. Enjoy what you're reading. And don't worry about hurrying through it. That would be like watching a show or movie at 2× speed or more. That's not cool.

This also goes for reading to kids. Crack open a good book. Read it out loud. And take your time.

3. Reading Religious Texts

The reading method below *does not* work well for religious texts. In fact, it defeats the purpose. Skim-reading is more about getting a high-level overview for maximum comprehension, whereas reading a religious text is geared toward life transformation—big difference.

When reading the Bible, for example, take your time. Don't worry about whether or not you read twenty chapters today or if you're on track to read the whole thing in a year. That's not the point (unless you're studying it for a class).

When You Should Read This Way

There are other times when you'll need or want to read a book—fast. Whether you're cramming for a presentation, preparing for an exam, writing a research paper or blog post, or are just looking for a few nuggets of wisdom and insight, you'll need to know how to devour a book as quickly as possible.

For whatever reason you want to read a book quickly, you can get the key insights from a small portion of what you read. How? Good nonfiction writing is structured in a particular way. And when you know this structure, you can grasp the big ideas with ease. Let us show you what we're talking about.

One Must-Know Tip before Skim-Reading

There's one key thing you must know before employing this method: the pattern most nonfiction writing follows. Knowing this pattern is like unlocking a secret code to accelerate your reading and comprehension. Here's the typical chapter-by-chapter format:

introduction

body

conclusion

Said another way, in good nonfiction, authors will tell you within each chapter what they're going to say (introduction), say it (body), and then tell you what they just said (conclusion).

Let's take a look at each of these in detail.

BRIAN WIELBIK, MARKET PRESIDENT AT FIRST COMMUNITY BANK MINOOKA/CHANNAHON/MORRIS, ON THE READING LIFE:

Michael Hyatt says, "What gets scheduled gets done." I schedule reading every day before bed from 9:30 to 10:30. I write down the name of what I am reading, the total pages in the book, what page number I want to read to that night, and the goal for pages to read. I am reading *The Splendid and the Vile* now and it looks like this: 508-425-10. Doing it this way gives me a sense of accomplishment. After finishing the book I log it into Goodreads and capture important information on a note card.

Introduction

The introduction of a chapter will include the key point an author wants to make. In a news story, this will be short and sweet to the tune of one or two thin paragraphs. In a book, the introduction of each chapter can be longer. Either way, in both of these scenarios, the writer lays out the most important information first—what you must know—with an enticing hook to whet your appetite to read more.

Body

After the introduction, nonfiction writers will move on to further explain what they've just shared. This can include additional details, background, and whatever relevant material they need to get their point across.

Here's one thing to know: the first sentence of paragraphs within the body will include the main point the author wants to make. After the first sentence, they'll then spend time explaining their point with stories, anecdotes, and examples. With this in mind, for most nonfiction writing you can read the first and last sentences of a paragraph to unearth its key message.

Conclusion

The conclusion will reiterate the author's main point from the introduction. If the conclusion is written well, the author will *not* present any new ideas. Rather, they will provide enough suspense to entice you to turn the page to the next chapter or make a poignant statement to bring their short piece to a close.

Now let's take a look at how you can use this information to skim a book fast to glean its most important details.

Three Steps to Reading a 220-Page Book in One Hour

It's time to get to work.[4] This three-step process will arm you with the tools you need to skim a book fast while unearthing the most essential information you need to know.

1. Get an Overview of the Book

Picking up a new book is a big commitment.

It can take several hours or more to read a book, and when you're unfamiliar with the book, you're not even sure if reading it will be worth your time or what you should take away. But you can reveal the unknown mysteries of a book by getting an overview, and here's how.

To get an overview of any nonfiction book, you'll want to read the book description, anything else on the front or back flap, and the introduction if available. Well-written book descriptions and/or the front or back flaps of book dust jackets will tell you in a few hundred words or less what the book is about, the benefits you'll receive from reading it, and a cliffhanger to motivate you to purchase it.

What is more, introductions will shed light on the author's motivation for writing the book and the author's goals for it. This peek under the hood lets you know what to expect from the book.

Finally, take a gander at the table of contents. How is the book broken down? Are there acknowledgments and an epilogue? Do the chapter titles clearly say what material will be covered? Reading the table of contents can give you the lay of the land, so to speak.

After reading this material, you'll possess a general overview of the book and know what to expect.

2. Break the Chapters Down into Time Blocks

Pacing yourself to read is essential to skimming a book in one hour.

For the sake of this exercise, look at the number of chapters in the book (not including the acknowledgments). To skim a book in one hour, how much time can you devote to every chapter? For example, if the book you're reading has ten chapters, you can devote six minutes per chapter.

Let's park here for a moment.

If you skip this step, then you'll end up spending forty-five minutes absorbing a few chapters but then blaze through the rest of the book. The result: an imbalanced understanding of the book. Pacing eliminates this problem. It allows you to give each essential topic equal attention.

3. Purposefully Skim-Read

"How in the world am I going to read a whole chapter in six minutes?"

That's a great question. In short, you're not going to be able to *read* a chapter that fast. Skimming in that amount of time, however, is quite doable.

Remember, nonfiction writing follows a specific structure, which is why skim-reading works—you're able to mine the most essential information by focusing on specific parts of a book.

In order to read one chapter in six minutes or less, you'll need to read

the introduction
the headings and subheadings
the first and last sentence of every paragraph
the conclusion

Skim-reading in this way will help you to grasp the big ideas of every chapter. If you have time left over, feel free to read additional material from that chapter or just move on to the next one.

Over to You

Hear us loud and clear: you don't want to read every book this way.

Whenever you approach a new book, determine your reading goals ahead of time. Then plan your reading accordingly. This way you can comprehend more in less time. And stockpile only the essential and vital ideas in your brain.

Further Reading

Daniel Kahneman's engaging *Thinking, Fast and Slow* provides a helpful analysis on how our brain thinks and forms thoughts, which provides more context on the lessons we shared both here and in the previous chapter on increasing your reading speed.

CHAPTER 11

How to Create an Unchangeable Reading Habit

*We can't become what we need to
by remaining what we are.*

Oprah Winfrey

Chandler Bolt was a C-level English student and college drop-out. It wasn't uncommon for him to be in honors classes in all but English because of his hatred (his word) for the reading and writing his English classes required.

When he dropped out of college, however, he decided to take what he calls a "college dropout's approach to learning." No longer would he read what he was assigned and eventually graded on. Instead, he'd put the responsibility to learn squarely on himself.

Though he was no longer attending school, Chandler said, "I treated life like I was still in school. I was going to miss the next two years of learning, so I needed to turn learning into a lifelong pursuit." What might that look like? He needed a mentor, he thought. But how would he even find a mentor? "The smartest, most successful people on the planet have put all the best things they've learned into a book," he reasoned. "And for $15 and a few hours of your time, you can learn from them."

Even a college dropout could afford what Chandler calls a "$15 mentor."

While Chandler didn't connect with the traditional school model and the books that came with his assignments, he *did* connect with other books, ones that piqued his curiosity and interest. Turns out he didn't hate reading after all. He just didn't like reading subjects he cared little about.

Today, Chandler has managed to work his way up to reading a book a week. Oh, and he's also written a few of his own. His success on that front even led to his founding an online education company devoted to teaching people how to write, market, and publish their first book.

Like Chandler, you too are not destined to be a non-reader.

You may have a learning disability. You may have struggled with English classes in school. Or you may be holding on to several excuses why you can't pick up a book. Whatever has influenced your ability or opinion about reading doesn't mean you can never form a reading habit.

Don't allow your struggles with reading or your self-imposed limitations to imprison you in a cell of fear. If you want to read, then read. A certain level of intelligence, ability to learn, or past reading experiences are not prerequisites for reading. Many successful readers and leaders did not become voracious readers until later in life.

There's no one holding you back. There's no angel you need to wait for to bless you with an exceptionally fast reading speed or a burning desire to read. And there's no past experience more powerful than your present-day opportunity to read and become the man or woman you desire to be.

But before you embark on this new journey, there's one step you must take first.

Remove Your Reading Obstacles

What has kept or is keeping you from reading? Take the time now to identify what holds you back.

Do you have a learning disability? Are you paralyzed by a limiting belief? Or have you listened to the lies of excuses for years? Whatever it is, uncover your reading obstacles, own them, seek help, and do whatever you have to do to create a reading habit.

As you identify your reading obstacles, you'll be able to overcome them.

Now it's time to work on creating your reading habit.

The Building Blocks of Habits

For better or worse, your habits are the most powerful influence in your life. They will lead you to become a better—or worse—person, friend, child, parent, spouse, employee, or reader. In many ways, they form the path to the life you live.

According to studies, habits make up about 40 percent of your daily activities.[1] This means that nearly half of what you do every day is habitual. Said another way, half of your day is done on autopilot—you just do what you do out of habit. Will Durant was spot-on when he said, "We are what we repeatedly do. Excellence then, is not an act, but a habit."[2]

In heeding Durant's advice, focus on forming a reading habit, not on how many books you want to read in a year.

When you develop a reading habit, a routine you regularly commit to every day or week, then the number of books you read will take care of itself.

To build an unchangeable reading habit, we'll follow the process laid out by James Clear in *Atomic Habits*.[3]

Every habit follows four fundamental steps: cue, craving, response, and reward. Let's take a look at these in detail. First, a *cue* serves as a signal that triggers a specific response. Cues can be tied to a specific time, location, push notification, text, family member, friend, coworker, and more. Second, *cravings* are the driving force fueling your habits—your motivation. Third, the *response* stage of a habit is the action itself. Finally, *reward* is the promise delivered by the response. Regardless of whether you have good or bad habits, they all follow this pattern.

Practically speaking, cues are seeing whatever reward you perceive, cravings are desiring the reward, and response is all about getting the reward. To see this in practice, let's take a look at one habit shared by the vast majority of adults in the United States: responding to a text or push notification. When you receive an alert on your phone (e.g., vibration, sound), you are cued. After receiving this cue, in general, you're going to crave the message. Upon feeling this motivation, you respond by getting your phone and reading whatever message you received. In the end, you reward yourself—you satisfy your craving—by reading the message and, consequently, getting your phone becomes associated with the alert on your phone.

To create a good habit—in this case, a reading habit—James Clear builds off of this foundation and suggests this process:

Step 1: make it obvious (cue).

Step 2: make it attractive (craving).

Step 3: make it easy (response).

Step 4: make it satisfying (reward).

In applying this advice to reading, here are some things to consider. For cues, two common options are time and location. Is there a particular time or day you can leverage as a cue? What about a location? Do you have a favorite spot in your home, your office, or a third space like a coffee shop that works well as a cue? Whatever cue you choose, make it crystal clear so there's no doubt in your mind what it is.

As for your craving, what is your desired reward? Is it to reduce your stress? What about getting better sleep? Or do you desire to become a better reader and leader? There are a ton of ways you can make your craving attractive. But let us also suggest leading yourself to crave the act of reading itself. At first, if you haven't read in a while, reading may not be enjoyable. But over time, reading is something you can grow to love and enjoy. When this happens, reading will be its own reward.

Finally, make reading as easy as possible. We've shared a ton of ideas and tips throughout this book. But there's one that bears repeating here: have access to a book at all times. This way, when you receive your cue and crave your reward, you will be able to satisfy your motivation with whatever book you read. Follow the steps laid out in chapter 7 to create a reading plan. Know what books you will read in the upcoming week and month and be sure to purchase or borrow them ahead of time. Creating a reading plan will keep you organized and focused and make it easier for you to form a reading habit.

With this in mind, let's get into the nitty-gritty details.

Create an Easy-to-Use Habit Tracker

Forming a reading habit is a marathon, not a sprint. According to a study published in the *European Journal of Social Psychology*, the median time it took participants to form a habit was sixty-six days.[4] It took some participants eighteen days to form a new habit, whereas it took other participants over two hundred days. We don't mean to discourage you with this news. Instead, we want to make sure you know what you're getting into so that you can prepare to succeed ahead of time.

On your path to developing a reading habit, there's one key tool you'll need: a habit tracker. There's nothing fancy about a habit tracker. It's simply a way you can keep track of your progress. This way you'll know whether or not you're on track to cultivating a reading habit.

Know why?

Tracking your progress works.

According to one weight loss study, participants who tracked what they ate daily lost twice as much weight compared to those who didn't keep a food journal.[5] The goodness associated with keeping track of what you do doesn't stop there. A recent study by the American Psychological Association discovered that people who track their progress toward a goal are more likely to succeed.[6]

What's the moral of the story?

Keeping track of how often you read will help you succeed. Remember, forming a reading habit will not happen overnight. You need to prepare yourself for the long haul. And one way to do that is by using a tracker, which serves as a proverbial map charting your course.

Don't make a complicated habit tracker. For starters, begin with whatever calendar you're already using to keep track of your daily, weekly, and monthly tasks. Within this calendar, add reading to the days you're going to read. For example, if you want to read Monday through Friday, add it to your calendar. After you've read, mark it complete. That's it!

If you don't use a calendar, no sweat. All you need is a piece of paper, an online calendar, or a physical journal to keep track of how often you read. Whatever option you choose, keep it simple. You don't want to spoil your reading efforts by getting hung up on how you're going to track your reading.

With your habit tracker in hand, now it's time to move on to adding how much you'll read throughout the month.

Start Small—Really Small

The key to beginning a new reading habit is to start small and build your way up. Your ability to do something, your willpower, is like a muscle. It can get fatigued during the day (binge eating at night, anyone?). It can be made stronger, and it can also grow weaker when not used.

When it comes to reading, if you currently don't read or read that often, then don't worry about creating a plan to read fifty, seventy-five, or more than a hundred books a year. At first, it's best to focus on reading a few pages or for a set time. Said another way, when you focus on the process of reading—reading specific pages or for a specific time—the number of books you read will take care of itself.

This is what I (Jeff) learned by happenstance. Today, I read dozens of books per year. But this wasn't always the case, I can assure you. Remember, I went twelve years without reading a single book.

Even after my love of reading was rekindled with the help of a book club, getting through just one book in a month seemed like a great accomplishment. And that's just it. It was! I had to work my way up slowly, reading one book per month, then two, three, and eventually four or more, depending upon the size of the books and my schedule.

This is one reason we suggest starting with a small reading goal. Make your goal so easy that it's nearly impossible to say no to. Instead of starting with fifty pages per day, begin with one to five pages. Don't worry about cranking out thirty minutes of reading every day. Start with one to five minutes.

Here's another way to start a small reading habit.

Let's say you want to read a two-hundred-page book in one month. If, for example, you know you'll be able to commit to reading on twenty days this month, simple math says you will only need to read ten pages per day to achieve your goal. That's totally doable, right?

Remember, your goal is to form a sustainable habit. By starting with a bite-sized goal, you'll make it easier on yourself to read and, in time, you'll form a lifelong reading habit.

This is one reason why I (Jeff) have grown to love the practice outlined by Dr. BJ Fogg in his book *Tiny Habits*.[7] To form a new habit, Dr. Fogg recommends breaking down your desired habit into the smallest steps possible. When it comes to creating a reading habit, this could mean reading one sentence, paragraph, or page at a time.

To reinforce this new behavior, add a celebratory moment afterward (an "air" high-five or a Tiger Woods–style fist pump, for example). Celebrating what you do has a way of convincing your brain that this action (what you just read) is one worth repeating. It's almost like giving yourself a Jedi mind trick.

When you celebrate, do so sincerely and exuberantly, as you naturally would for any other achievement. It will feel cheesy at first. And that's okay. You're telling your brain that what you did (reading) is something that makes you feel good.

Don't stress about starting your new reading habit from scratch.

Identify one thing (habit) you do every day you can leverage to get yourself to read. This is what Dr. Fogg calls an "anchor," and what James Clear refers to as "habit stacking." For example, are you a coffee drinker who never misses your morning cup? Great; use this habit as an anchor for reading. It could go something like this: "After I start the coffee maker (anchor), I will read one page (new habit). When I'm done, I will pump my fist in the air (celebration)."

When starting a new habit, if you on occasion don't read, that's okay. Get back on the horse the next day. Ideally, you just don't want to miss two days in a row. But if you do, don't count your efforts lost. Just get back at it.

There's one more thing we'd like to point out: if your original goal, such as reading five pages per day, isn't happening, don't be afraid to revise your plans. Maybe you need to reduce your goal to reading one page per day or for one minute. It's okay to adapt your plans.

Remember, big things have small beginnings. It doesn't matter how little you read at first. What matters is that you consistently read to form a reading habit. Besides, you can increase how much and how often you read at a later date when you're ready.

Practically speaking, decide if you're going to read daily or on certain days during the week. Figure out either how many pages you want to read or for how long you're going to keep your nose in a book on the days you read. Add this task to your calendar and your habit tracker, and you'll be one big step closer to forming a reading habit.

Seek Private and Public Accountability

Don't believe you're on your own in starting a new reading habit. There's no universal principle that says you have to be a Lone Ranger. It's actually a good idea to seek private and public accountability, encouragement, and support along the way.

According to a variety of surveys and studies, having someone hold you accountable is one of the leading factors when it comes to accomplishing your goals. Someone who can encourage you, challenge you, and pick you up when you fall down.

Having someone hold you accountable is more than texting them for help. It involves sharing your goals with someone, giving them permission to hold you responsible for meeting them, and agreeing to some sort of schedule to check in on your progress. When you do this, you're placing yourself in a better spot to overcome whatever challenge you face in forming your reading habit. In a sense, the people you surround yourself with will serve as a gravitational force pulling you forward toward success.

Find someone who's willing to support you, such as a friend, family member, coworker, or spouse. Share your reading plan with them and let them know the steps you're going to take. Inform them how often you plan on reading. This way, the two of you will be clear on what's expected. What is more, it's best if this person is a reader too. Partnering with someone who's already a reader will go a long way toward helping you to achieve your goals.

In addition to having a personal confidant to hold you accountable, consider sharing your goals publicly, including on social media. For full disclosure, we haven't been too transparent about our personal goals on social media. But according to a variety of weight loss studies, publicly sharing your goals can improve your progress.[8] Researchers have discovered that when participants in a weight loss program shared their progress and posted it on social media, they lost more weight compared to those who kept the progress they made to themselves. Sharing how much you're going to read and what you're reading can fuel your progress toward building a reading habit.

Starting a new reading habit is challenging. But you're not required to go about it alone. Before you face any setbacks

AL COMEAUX, AUTHOR OF *CHANGE THE MANAGEMENT*, ON THE READING LIFE:

I was working at Travelocity when I read a brand-new book called *Good to Great* by Jim Collins. I began to wonder, along with others, what our "hedgehog concept" was. What can we be the best in the world at? Through this and other books that followed, the idea for a Travelocity customer guarantee took off. Now fifteen years, two owners, and an unknown number of CEOs later, the guarantee is still standing as Travelocity's differentiator in the marketplace . . . its hedgehog concept.

or discouragement in this process, commit to finding an accountability partner or publicly sharing your progress. In doing so, you'll surround yourself with the added support you'll need to accomplish your goals.

Why Your Reading Habit Is Something You Should Never Stop

When I (Jeff) first launched the *Read to Lead* podcast in July 2013, I envisioned my listener as someone who'd found themselves, career-wise, in the same place I was ten or so years earlier—with a decent job and life but nothing amazing to "write home about." Through my podcast, I would convince them how quickly they could expand their influence and boost their career using the same simple process I had used: intentional and consistent reading.

This is an accurate description of many of my listeners in those early days. But a funny thing happened along the way. As I began to offer programs that grew out of the show, such as one-on-one coaching, mastermind groups, and a book club, I began to notice a trend. The people I was attracting to these programs through my podcast weren't just folks early in their careers looking to up their game. It was people who were, in the eyes of most, *already* successful: presidents, CEOs, pastors, entrepreneurs, nonprofit leaders, and board members. In other words, people who not only recognized the importance of reading as part of their plan *toward* achieving success but also realized that reading would be crucial in helping them *stay* that way.

One of my favorite authorities on leadership, John Maxwell, says, "Far too often, leaders drift. Once they get some experience under their belt and a track record of accomplishments, they often abandon the lifestyle that helped them reach the top."[9] My podcast was reaching, and seemingly speaking to, the kinds of leaders who were self-aware enough to know they couldn't afford to drift. They couldn't rest on their laurels. They needed to remain sharp.

This is true of us all.

We need to remain sharp. There will never be a time when we "arrive." We'll never get to a point in life where we'll know everything, have all of the answers, or never need to hear a different perspective. Reading plays a big part in keeping our edge.

Growing professionally is an ongoing process. As soon as you're convinced you don't need to read, learn, or grow, you won't. If anything, your cognitive abilities will decline as you age if you avoid reading.

Over to You

When you miss a reading day, don't give up. Just pick up wherever you left off. Getting back on track and picking up a book to read is a big difference between a lifelong reader and everyone else. They don't get hung up on how much they did or didn't read. They simply continue to move forward, expressing their love for the written word by reading.

Further Reading

Dig deeper into creating life-giving habits by reading

Atomic Habits: An Easy & Proven Way to Build Good Habits & Break Bad Ones by James Clear

The Power of Habit: Why We Do What We Do in Life and Business by Charles Duhigg

Tiny Habits: The Small Changes That Change Everything by BJ Fogg

CHAPTER 12

The Key to (Nearly) Mastering Anything

> When you sell a man a book, you don't sell him 12 ounces
> of paper and ink and glue—you sell him a whole new life.
>
> *Christopher Morley*

For most of my career, I (Jeff) worked in live radio. Anytime I turned on my microphone, I was speaking to thousands of people. So you'd think I'd have felt comfortable with public speaking, right? Well, you'd be wrong.

Even though I've addressed rooms of hundreds of people—even thousands in recent years—there was a time when I dreaded giving public presentations. It's one thing to be on the radio, hiding behind a mic and knowing people can only hear you, not see you. It's a completely different ball game, for me at least, to be on a stage in front of people.

So how did I change? I identified my problem, demystified the process, and worked to improve my public presentations. Let me explain.

Once I made the decision that public speaking was a skill I wanted and needed to unlock, I knew books held the key. I began with titles about presentation design. *Presentation Zen* by Garr Reynolds and *Slideology* by Nancy Duarte were two of my early reads. Were I to do it over, I'd likely not start with design but rather structure and delivery. Still, these specific books helped me gain confidence. I found that when I felt good about my slides and knew I had illustrated my points in a compelling way, I was far less nervous on stage.

My desire to learn more about this art was brought on by the success I was having in other areas of my job, made possible in large part by what I was reading about leadership, marketing, and the customer experience. I was being invited more and more to share my thoughts, experiments, and findings.

When I later made the transition to working for myself, I read *Steal the Show* by Michael Port, *Secrets of Dynamic Communication* by Ken Davis, *Fearless Speaking* by Gary Genard, *Talk Like TED* by Carmine Gallo, *Resonate* by Nancy Duarte, *The Successful Speaker* by Grant Baldwin with Jeff Goins, *The Compelling Communicator* by Tim Pollard, *Mastering the Art of Public Speaking* by Michael J. Gelb, and others. Each one of these books helped me to hone specific skills within the realm of public speaking.

In 2018, after delivering a talk to a room of about 450 authors (a group of creators who have had a significant influence on me and my career), I received my first ever standing ovation. I share this to help you understand how far I've come. If I can go from terrible to tolerable, and eventually even to terrific (at least in the eyes of some) in one area of my life, then so can you . . . for nearly any skill you desire to master.

Improving yourself professionally isn't something you can take for granted. Nor is it something you can place on the proverbial back burner forever. You must strive to learn new skills, gain new insight, and boost your strengths.

Here's why.

It's Easy to Fall Behind

Complacency and the status quo can solidify like slow-setting cement. Before you know it, you're stuck, you can't move, and your only option is to take whatever help is available. It doesn't matter if you're in your twenties, thirties, or forties, or are on the verge of retirement. This can happen to anyone.

You see, the world we live in is changing—fast. Businesses come and go. Career changes are common. And you're competing with countless others in the marketplace.

You cannot stand still.

You have to focus on making forward progress.

You must continue to set new goals, learn new skills, and gain wisdom.

If you don't take action, then your peers and competitors will leave you behind. In the words of Lou Holtz, a College Football Hall of Fame head coach, "In this world you're either growing or you're dying, so get in motion and grow."[1] This is more than a rah-rah speech from an impassioned football coach. There's merit to his words.

As we pointed out in chapter 1, the average employee tenure is 4.6 years, and the life expectancy of a company on the S&P 500 is barely fifteen years. Seeing that neither employee tenure nor businesses last forever, if you're not staying ahead of the game, your time is running out or your company's profitability will soon be over.

That's not all.

According to a study by the Pew Research Center, 74 percent of adults in the United States identified themselves as personal learners, meaning that within the last year they read a book, took a course, or attended a meeting or event to learn more.[2] At a minimum, this means if you're not doing the same, then you'll eventually get passed by.

Taking action on what we share in this book will help you stay sharp. But if you want to accelerate your growth, then stick around. Below, we're going to walk you through the process of (nearly) mastering any topic, acquiring new skills, and creating new opportunities.

Know Your "Why"

First of all, clarify your purpose and goals. Simply having an interest in studying a topic isn't enough. You have to possess a compelling reason *why* to fuel your work. Moving forward with this plan of study without a purpose is like starting a road trip without a destination—you'll aimlessly meander around and never reach an intended goal.

Why do you want to study a topic?

What's your purpose?

It's easy to confuse your purpose with your goals. But the answer to this question—why—is the reason *behind* what you want to accomplish. It's what backs up what you want to do. For example, learning how to do something new, become a better manager, and improve your communication skills are what you want to accomplish. These are your goals. But answering why you want to accomplish these goals will propel you toward accomplishing them.

Not sure why you want to do something?

Keep asking yourself why until you arrive at the root of your goals. You may need to ask two to five times or more. Keep asking yourself this same question until you're able to place your fingers on the pulse of your purpose.

Focus on One Topic

Pick one topic you want to master.

Whatever topic you choose, focus your reading on knowing it inside and out. Be sure to nail down your choice, because it will guide your actions in the following steps.

When thinking about a topic, there are probably a few options that come to mind. Narrow down your choices to one topic you want to or need to focus on to grow personally or professionally.

Interested in becoming a better spouse or parent? There are truckloads of these types of books available. Need to fill some gaps in your knowledge at work? You'll have plenty of books to choose from. Curious to know how to best lead and manage people? You'll have to swim through a sea of books to find the right one.

Whatever focal point you choose, be specific and fight for clarity as you set your goals. For instance, "I want to become a better marketer" is vague, lacks a deadline, and isn't connected to any purpose. "To become a better marketer and obtain a promotion, I will become an expert in consumer behavior and sales, master Facebook advertising, and get certified in Google Analytics and Google Ads in twelve months" ties in to a purpose, specifies exactly what you need to learn, and delineates the time needed to accomplish this goal.

In spelling out your plan, follow the SMART goals framework to focus your efforts. A SMART goal is Specific, Measurable, Achievable, Relevant, and Time-Based.

Take whatever time you need on this step. It's at this point you must clarify what you need to know. Afterward, you'll be ready to plan your method of attack, which leads us to the next step.

Make Micro-Goals

There's only one way to accomplish any task or goal that'll take longer than five minutes: take it one step at a time. Practically speaking, you'll need to take your topic and break it down into smaller pieces that can become your SMART goals. Any topic you choose will include multiple components. Think about what all is involved in becoming better in any of these areas:

life	parenting
friendship	managing
marriage	social media
marketing	leading
theology	entrepreneurship
business	engineering
finances	construction

Before you pick one book to read, break down your topic into smaller pieces. To get started, identify the qualities, knowledge, and skills that make up the topic you picked. Do a little research. Jot down your notes. And see if you can identify seven to ten different components. After you complete this step, you're ready to move on.

Create Your Own Curriculum

Don't be intimidated by the sound of this.

Here, you're just taking the different components you identified above and picking a book to read for each specific topic. Basically, you'll end up with seven to ten books to read. That's it.

SETH GODIN, AUTHOR OF TWENTY BESTSELLING BOOKS, INCLUDING *THE PRACTICE*, ON THE READING LIFE:

Books are special for a few reasons. The first one is that they have a Proustian impact on a lot of people who were lucky enough to grow up the way I did, which is they represent curation and thoughtfulness. I mean, no one writes a book in ten minutes.

And for other people it's a problem because it reminds them of discipline in school and being bored, which is why most people in the United States only read one or two books a year, which is astonishing and sad.

But the other thing a book does in the nonfiction world is it's all of it in one place. That's not the way a blog post works. That's not how a YouTube video works. Here it is in one place.

I can hand it to someone else.

And so the reason I bother with books—I can reach way more people with a blog post—is because I want someone who receives a book to give it to someone else. Because ideas that are spread, that are shared, change our culture, and they do it in a concentrated form, not widely, but in pockets.

We know this doesn't sound like a ton of books. But reading multiple books on one topic will actually put you way ahead of the game in the United States. Here's why:

- Read one book on a topic, and you'll know more than 27 percent of US adults, who haven't read a book in the past year.[3]
- Read five books on a topic, and you'll know more than the average American, who has only read four books in the past year.[4]
- Read ten or more books on a topic, and there's a good chance you'll know more than 99 percent.

In context, it doesn't take reading dozens of books to be well informed on any topic. Of course, we're not talking about how many books you'll need to read to obtain your bachelor's degree, master's degree, or PhD. Getting a degree is a totally different ball game. The idea here is doing what you can to educate yourself.

Stick with the loose guidelines we provide here. Initially planning on reading more books may lead you down the wrong path. Give yourself permission to read a handful of books on your topic and then adapt your plan if you want to pursue a different angle. Depending upon how familiar you are with your topic, there's a good chance you'll get interested in something specific along the way. So give yourself the freedom to pursue those paths as they open up before you.

Not sure what you should read? To get started, try one or more of these tips:

- Search for popular books on the topic.
- Look for authors you're familiar with.

- See what other books authors reference in their books.
- Follow recommendations from authors.
- Search for books online.
- Ask for someone's suggestion.

For more help in formulating a reading plan, check out chapter 7.

Don't start reading through your pile of books yet. There's something important you need to prepare yourself for first.

Summarize What You Read

Summarizing your reading is like injecting your learning with jet fuel—it'll accelerate your progress (we cover this in more detail in chapter 8). Sure, you can get away without doing it. Reading a lot of books alone will influence your thinking. Peep Laja, the founder and principal of CXL, shared how reading multiple books on one topic evolved his thinking and provided him with more depth and nuance.[5] But summarizing what you read has proven scientific benefits you don't want to miss.

According to research, summarizing a book will help you to retain 50 percent more of what you read compared to those who don't do it. As you look through your notes, identify key points, and summarize your findings, you're really digesting a book and absorbing it into your bloodstream.

That's not all. Writing book summaries provides several other benefits, including

clarifying your thoughts about the book
revealing your gaps in knowledge

making your notes easily accessible

helping you connect ideas from different books

saving time when retrieving your notes and thoughts

improving your writing, which is an essential communication skill

Naturally, you're probably wondering how to write a book summary or how long this process takes. To be honest, there's not a one-size-fits-all approach. It all depends on what you want to get out of the books you read.

James Clear, author of *Atomic Habits*, writes a three-sentence summary of the main idea, pulls interesting quotes, and jots down miscellaneous thoughts. Tiago Forte, one of the world's foremost experts on productivity, will spend upwards of ten to twenty hours summarizing select books. From these two examples alone, you can see there's a huge variety in how to summarize a book.

As you think about what will work best for you, keep these questions in mind:

- What's the book about?
- What is the main idea of every chapter?
- How does the author prove their point?
- What do you find helpful?
- What do you disagree with?
- What is something you can act upon?
- How does this book compare to a different book?

Go to readtoleadbook.com/resources to download a book summary checklist.

- Are there common themes you've identified between books?
- Are there quotes and ideas you want to save?

You don't have to answer all of these questions. We're just sharing a smattering of ideas you can consider when writing a book summary that meets your needs.

Reinforce Your Reading

Reinforcing your reading will cement what you learn. Again, many studies and surveys, and a depth of historical examples validate multiple ways you can learn something new.

Without personally knowing you, it's hard to say what will work best for you. Depending on what you've set out to accomplish, here are sixteen ways you can accelerate your learning.[6]

1. Break down what you need to learn into the smallest possible parts.[7]
2. Practice, practice, and practice.
3. Change how you practice.[8]
4. Get feedback.
5. Seek out a mentor or coach.
6. Focus on learning one skill at a time.
7. Test yourself.[9]
8. Teach someone else what you learned.
9. Get more sleep and take naps.
10. Regularly exercise.
11. Study or practice in short bursts.[10]

12. Say out loud what you want to learn.[11]
13. Watch videos.
14. Read articles.
15. Immerse yourself in experiences.
16. Take courses online or on campus.

Thankfully, you don't have to do everything on this list. For what it's worth, we recommend focusing on practicing, getting feedback, and seeking out a mentor or coach who can hold you accountable and push you beyond your comfort zone. Combining these three tactics along with your reading will be a booster shot for your personal and professional development.

Take Action

You made it!

You've set a goal, read your books, summarized your reading, and reinforced what you've read in a variety of ways. Unless you set out on this path only for the sake of gaining wisdom, it's time to put your hard work into action.

As we pointed out in chapter 8, the one thing a book—as well as an online course, coach, or degree—cannot do for you is *take the action*. No one and nothing else can take what you learn and put it into practice. Only you have the power to put your new knowledge and skills to work.

Feel more confident with digital advertising? Seek out an opportunity to show off your new skills. Know what you want to say in a presentation? It's time to put your thoughts to paper—or a PowerPoint or Keynote presentation. Ready to take on management opportunities at work? Start to put into practice the lessons you've learned.

Over to You

Put what you've learned into action or take a break from the books if you must. But don't stop there. There's more to learn, new skills to acquire, and adventures to experience. Pick a new topic and rinse and repeat the same process above. Over the course of time, you'll have (nearly) mastered multiple topics, grown personally and professionally, and, with the wealth of knowledge you've obtained, you'll be the center of dinnertime conversations.

Further Reading

Take the lessons from this chapter one step further (and more) by reading

Mastery by Robert Greene

Talent is Overrated: What Really Separates World-Class Performers from Everybody Else by Geoff Colvin

Outliers by Malcolm Gladwell

CHAPTER 13

Fifteen Tips on How to Read Smarter

Lack of direction, not lack of time, is the problem.
We all have 24-hour days.

Zig Ziglar

Every house has at least one "junk" or "catchall" drawer. A drawer in the kitchen, bedroom, or office that's full of random stuff. Infrequently used cords, screwdrivers, or small objects that have no other home are some of the things you'll find in one of my (Jesse's) drawers.

Not everything in them is necessarily junk. These drawers are normally full of items we haven't organized yet or, if we're being honest, maybe never will. This doesn't devalue what's in them. If anything, an item in one of these drawers could be the most valuable thing in our home (car keys, anyone?).

Think of this chapter like our "catchall" chapter.

It's chock-full of miscellaneous tips to help you read smarter, become more well-informed, and better live the reading life.

The tips below aren't in any particular order. So feel free to bound about in a puppy-like manner.

1. Reread All Sorts of Books

There's a good chance your "to be read" pile of books is a mile high by now. Books you want to read for work, to improve your relationships, or for sheer entertainment. Besides, the thrill of picking up a new book, buying it, and then dropping it in your "to read" pile is intoxicating. But there are times you'll want to hit the pause button on reading something new and, instead, reread a book.

This may strike you as odd or counterproductive. But there are several reasons why you should consider rereading books, and many people throughout history have done the same. From Charles Spurgeon rereading *The Pilgrim's Progress* by John Bunyan more than one hundred times[1] to Warren Buffett sharing how often he's read *The Intelligent Investor* by Benjamin Graham, stories of people rereading books are in abundance, and for good reason too.[2]

Rereading books can improve your comprehension, reground you in something you value, or show you something you missed before. As time passes and you reread books, you'll see new things because, in a sense, you're a new person. You have lived more life and gained wisdom, which means you're sitting down with an old book with a new perspective.

After numerous failed attempts in the past, I (Jeff) managed last year to finally make reading from my Bible a daily practice. As I am someone who's been reading the Bible off and on since I was five, it is not hard to imagine how often I've reread certain passages over the years.

This was never more the case for me than it was in recent years. Having managed to make it through the entire Bible over the course of the year, I eventually reread everything I'd ever read in the past. But now with a few more years of living under my belt, and hopefully a bit more wisdom, even the verses I was quite familiar with often took on new meaning.

This is one of the strongest arguments to me for rereading any book that resonates with you. As you grow and stretch personally and professionally, you naturally gain new perspectives. These experiences serve almost like a fresh pair of eyes when coming back to a book a second, third, or even fourth time.

2. Read until You Love It

Reading isn't a natural activity enjoyed by all. For a variety of reasons, there are people who have loved reading from birth, others who could take it or leave it, and some who'd never dream about cracking open a book. Regardless of where you fall on this spectrum, reading books is something you can grow to love. But your love for reading may not come easy—it will require effort, discipline, and perseverance.

You see, reading books isn't a passive experience like sitting back, eating popcorn, and binge-watching your favorite television show. Instead, reading actively requires your focus, attention, and physically turning the page, swiping over to the next page on your e-reader, or scrolling down the page.

In sharing this with you, we want to let you know what you're getting into and that you will face resistance when you begin to read more books. When this happens, decide in your heart to pick up a book, even if only for a few minutes, and force yourself to read it like you love it. In time, as you read, you will grow in your love for reading. You may just have to fake it until you make it at first.

3. Save Things to Read for Later

Fact: it's impossible to read everything that has been or will be written.

Know what else?

You'll never be able to read everything you want to read. Now, we are not curmudgeons who are here to dash your dreams against the rocks. Instead, we want to help you focus on reading material that'll help you to learn new skills, expand your influence, and boost your career.

What's the point? You're going to stumble upon something you want to read nearly every day, and you're not going to have the time to read it right then and there. So get ready to keep a list of what you want to read later.

For me (Jesse), I randomly started using a Wishlist on Amazon to keep track of books I may want to read later. What is more, when I see an interesting article online, I'll use a "Read It Later" app, an RSS Reader tool like Feedly, or perhaps a Web Clipper to save it for later.

Having a plan in place today to save something to read for later will be a stress-saver.

4. Always Carry (or Have Access to) a Book

Having access to a book at all times is a game-changer. You'll be surprised by how many times during the day you'll be able to read.

Is someone late to your meeting? Read a book. Sitting in traffic? Scan a page. Taking a train, subway, or bus to the city? Breeze through a few chapters. This one reading habit will boost the number of books you can read.

Know what else? Carrying a book with you is one way you can reduce your stress and better enjoy your commutes; it can be a conversation starter, or, if you'd prefer not to talk to anyone, it's a great way to avoid people too (if you fall into this latter camp, you can thank us later).

5. Don't Only "Read" Summaries

Traditional book summaries have been around as long as books have been written. Entire businesses have been built on creating summaries and study guides for books (think CliffsNotes). Summaries or curated insights are helpful supplements. But summaries are not replacements for reading and are not to be confused with reading books—they're obviously different.

As we laid out in chapter 2, there are a number of scientific benefits to reading, but you will not experience these same benefits by reading summaries written by someone else. Also, summaries are just that—they summarize the key points of a book. They are helpful tools for supporting your reading habit and can be great in a pinch if you only need to glean a few points. But don't sell yourself short by only reading or listening to summaries. This is like chewing on a piece of nutritious food and then spitting it out—you'll only enjoy the taste but not benefit from the substance.

For a list of recommended tools, go to readtoleadbook.com/resources.

6. Get the Most out of Audiobooks Three Ways

Retaining what you hear from audiobooks can be challenging. Whether you're driving your car to work or listening to something while multitasking, remembering what you hear is tough.

When I (Jeff) began listening to audiobooks during my commute, I found that my mind often wandered off into deep thought on the topic just presented. I was usually three or four minutes into pondering my thoughts before I'd realize I'd missed the last few minutes of what the narrator said. This can be frustrating, as you're having to hit the back button a few times to figure out where it was your mind left off. Over time, I managed to develop a work-around. I didn't want to stop my mind from "wandering off" into thought because, more often than not, I was thinking more deeply about what the author had just shared, which is another way of saying I was already trying to think of ways I might apply what I'd just learned. That's a good thing, right?

When this happened, I began to practice pausing the audiobook the moment I started ideating. Now I give myself the freedom to think through my idea or application to an obvious conclusion. Only after I feel my brain is done do I hit the play button and restart the audiobook.

Granted, it takes longer to get through an audiobook this way. But it's better than missing major portions of a book because your brain is trying to do two things at once (which we know is impossible).

Another way you can better retain what you hear is by using the clip or bookmark function in your favorite audiobook platform. For example, with Audible, you can use their Audible Clip function, which will save the passage you're listening to. When you come across something you want to revisit, save your spot and then pick it up later. This way you can relisten to the passage and take notes if you'd like.

Now that you know you can save key spots and revisit them later, the next way you can get the most out of audiobooks is by increasing the narrator's speed. Remember, you can read faster than you talk, which means you can also listen faster than you speak.

Don't feel like you have to listen to audiobooks at the fastest rate available. We know the allure of being able to listen to a six-hour audiobook in two hours by increasing the speed to 3× is tempting. But let's be honest: you won't comprehend or retain much of anything if you do this. However, you can increase the speed to a rate you're comfortable with.

First, increase the narrator's speed to 1.25× and see how it works for you. Afterward, pump it up to 1.5× to see if you're able to still comprehend what you're listening to. For me (Jesse), I like to warm up a bit by listening to an audiobook at the normal rate, then increase to 1.5×. This normally works well for me. But there are times I have to scale it back a bit because I'm unable to keep up.

7. Read Books to Help Solve Problems

What we're about to say will set you free: you do not have to read every book on whatever "top" reading list you stumble upon. For nearly every topic, you can find a list of the top-selling or best-ranking books. Sure, there are books on these lists you can benefit from. But reading a list of recommended books may not do you a lick of good because it is a general list for a general audience—not you in particular.

Instead, pick up a book that will help you solve a specific problem, take advantage of a new opportunity, or assist you in developing a new skill. For example, I (Jesse) recently read several books on sales to better inform my thinking in this area in my line of work, which is marketing. Reading these books informed my viewpoint and helped me to solidify my plans and get to work.

I (Jeff) have read almost twenty books on the topic of public speaking and creating great presentations. This is a skill I desire to excel at. Because of this, I find reading books on this topic to be fun and something I always look forward to. And I know I'm doing something most public speakers don't do, which gives me an advantage.

Mind you, I realize the fastest way to get better at something is to actually do it; in my case, I give presentations as often as I can. However, my reading on this topic is helping to teach me things like effective storytelling, best practices with regard to structure and flow, getting clearer on my message, dealing with things like anxiety, and lots more.

MICHAEL HYATT, *NEW YORK TIMES* BESTSELLING AUTHOR AND FOUNDER OF LEADERBOOKS, ON THE READING LIFE:

I don't read for retention. I read for stimulation, for assimilation, for innovation, for a lot of reasons. I don't care if I can recount exactly what that author said, but it's the synthesis that I get in my own brain as I read. And that creates an ROI because new ideas are what spawn new services, new products, everything good that happens in my business.

Don't stress yourself out by forcing yourself to read every book on every list. Use these "top" lists for ideas on what to read, but choose what appears to be most helpful to you.

8. Five Tips for Reading E-Books

Many of the lessons we've shared in this book are applicable to reading e-books with your smartphone or tablet. However, there are a few tips only for reading e-books you'll need to know.

For starters, when it comes to guiding your reading with a pointer (as we talked about in chapter 9), you cannot use your finger on a tablet or mobile device. Instead, you'll need to use something else to pace your reading, such as a pen, the eraser end of a pencil, or a stick (okay, we're joking about this last option).

Second, play around with different fonts. Not every available font is created equal, and some are better suited for reading e-books. Fonts in the sans serif family are considered ideal. But find a font that works best for you on a tablet or smartphone.

Third, decrease the brightness of your screen and experiment with different backgrounds. One of the primary causes of eyestrain is the background lighting you choose. Decrease the brightness of your screen to see if it helps, use a dark background with light font, or experiment with different screen dimming apps.

Fourth, one area in which e-books excel is highlighting and notes. As you read, you can easily make highlights and jot down your notes. Later, you can export your highlights and notes if you'd prefer to organize them in one spot.

Fifth, turn on the continuous scroll option. This enables you to seamlessly read by effortlessly scrolling down your screen versus swiping to the next page. This way you won't lose your place and you'll save yourself seconds per swipe. This might not sound like much, but it quickly adds up—especially if you're reading on a smartphone with a smaller screen compared to a tablet or e-reader.

These five tips should increase your reading speed, help you to retain what you read, and give you a more enjoyable reading experience with e-books.

9. Don't Look for *the* Book

Getting married and choosing what book to read have one thing in common: you're saying yes to one person or book and saying no to billions of other people and millions of books. So, yeah, we understand the pressure when it comes to choosing what to read. Besides, it's hard to commit to a book you'll potentially spend several hours consuming, and you really have no idea whether or not it'll be worth even five minutes of your time until you start digging in.

Anyhow, don't put too much stress on yourself about choosing "the book"—one that will change your life. In time, as you read, you will stumble upon books that will make a tremendous impact upon your life. What Tyler Cowen calls a "quake book," something that shakes you to the core.[3] In life, you will read books that will give you a new perspective, fill you with inspiration and hope, and lead you to live a happier, healthier, and fuller life. But you're not *necessarily* going to find this book on someone else's reading list. Books that changed someone else's life may end up collecting dust on your bookshelf. We're not saying you shouldn't read books recommended by someone else. We just want to let you know that a life-changing book will find you in the course of your reading pursuits.

Know what else?

Don't feel bad if you don't get a lot out of the books you read. Truth be told, not every word in every book—including this one—contains earth-shattering wisdom or ongoing entertainment. Be open to allowing an idea, a chapter, a paragraph, or even one sentence from a book to change your life. Walking away from a book with just *one* inspirational, helpful, or mind-changing thought is worth more than the few dollars you shelled out for purchasing it.

10. Buy as Many Books as You Can (Reasonably) Afford

Reading is a common habit shared by many successful people today and throughout history. It's responsible for unlocking limitless creativity and influence. It's been the inspiration for countless generations in creating tremendous impact. It's known to reduce stress, improve your decision-making skills, and make you a better leader. So what should you do? Buy as many books as you can, of course.

Buy books you want to read.
Buy books you'll partially read.
Buy books you think you'll read.
Buy books you may never read.

Build a library. Leave books on your nightstand, at work, in your living room, and in your bathroom (there, we said it). Surround yourself with books.

We're not suggesting for you to turn into a bibliomaniac—someone who obsessively hoards books to the point of financial ruin and social isolation. Rather, we believe it's best to surround yourself with all sorts of books.

For starters, having access to books will make it easier for you to read. Feel tempted to watch too much TV? Keep a stack of books next to the remote. Have a hard time falling asleep? Leave a few of your favorite nighttime books on your nightstand. Have a favorite spot you sit in your home? Keep a few books close by.

Stockpiling physical books in the house isn't new or trendy. It's a universal ideal, and it's been around for years. In Japan, stockpiling books you may never read is called *tsundoko*, and the idea dates back to the mid-nineteenth century, when books would have been more difficult to come by.

"I don't see the point in buying so many books," you may say.

That's a fair point, and you may not agree with what we're about to share, but here we go: surrounding yourself with books you have not read and may never read will keep you humble and curious. Nassim Nicholas Taleb, author of *The Black Swan*, said your library "should contain as much of what you do not know as your financial means, mortgage rates and the currently tight real-estate market allow you to put there."[4]

The sight of books you haven't read or have only partially read will be a subtle reminder that you haven't learned nor can learn everything there is to know. You'll find this subtle reminder isn't one of shame and guilt. Instead, it'll keep you hungry and searching to learn and grow more as a person and professional.

11. Read More Than One Book at a Time, If You Want To

"I have to read one book at a time."

This is a common myth, and one you don't have to believe in. Unless you need to read a book for class, work, or a specific project, there's no reason you cannot stop reading a book, pick up another title that's more intriguing in the moment, and return later to whatever book you just put down.

Reading multiple books at once is actually a good thing. You can switch between reading books you have to or want to read with something you find more enjoyable. You don't have to force yourself to read something you're not enjoying in the moment.

When you're reading a book from which you want to wring out every idea and lesson, there's a certain level of attention you have to provide to do this. Now, say you're hanging out at lunch, taking a break from work, or getting ready for bed; you're not going to be in the best spot physically to be as active a reader as you'd like for that particular book. So reading multiple books at once is a more natural way to read. It's one way to go along with the rhythms of your life. Don't pressure yourself to read one book at a time until it's finished. That's a fool's errand you don't have to run.

12. Share What You Learn

As you read, you'll be struck by certain ideas. Some will cause you to pause and ponder, while other ideas will strike you like a bolt of lightning. When you are struck with something you feel is significant, it'll challenge what you believe or the work you do, or even help you to connect several dots together. Regardless of how small or significant an idea that strikes you is, one way you can forge this new thought into your thinking is to share it with others.

There are many ways you can share your ideas. This can be one-on-one in a conversation, by 280 characters in a tweet, or through a blog post, to name a few. Kevin Hendricks, an author, journalist, and prolific reader, said, "When I find something engaging, I blog about it. The act of sharing what I've learned is one of the best ways to cement something."[5] To Kevin's point, you can go deep into one idea in what you're reading. Or you can summarize your thoughts about a whole book to help you retain what you've read. Your book summaries can be personal, or you can publish them online, which is a common practice among many, including James Clear, Nat Eliason, and Tiago Forte.

For me (Jeff), sharing what I've learned with others around me over the years has greatly increased my ability to not only retain what I've read but also challenge my "findings." Sharing invites others to offer their opinions. Sometimes, that leads to things I never would have thought of otherwise. Heck, part of my motivation for starting the *Read to Lead* podcast was the ability it offered me to share with others on a regular basis what I was reading and enjoying.

The act of sharing what you're learning forces you to understand what you're reading to the point that you can share it with others in whatever format or medium you choose. As you share the ideas you're learning from the books you read, you'll be able to better retain the lessons you learn along the way.

As we've shared in chapter 8, engage the books you read. Make marks. Highlight interesting thoughts. Summarize what you're reading. And in the end, share what you're reading with others to force yourself to learn from the books you read.

13. Use Deadlines to Read More and Faster

Deadlines in reading are helpful in two ways.

First, as we shared in chapter 9, it's ideal to read in short blocks of time. Even though your brain isn't technically a muscle, it should be treated like one. At some point during your reading, you'll get tired, and your reading speed and comprehension will decline. When you're reading to learn, use deadlines. Challenge yourself to read as much as you can within a certain period of time. Over time, using a deadline will help you to read more pages and books.

Second, use deadlines to increase how many words per minute you read. Regardless of your average wpm, regularly challenge yourself to read faster. Treating your reading like something you need to improve will lead you to train for it like a race. Every few weeks or month or so, schedule time to test your reading speed. Keep doing this until you're happy with how fast you can read while comprehending what you read.

14. Read to Understand Groups of Words

We hit on this a bit in chapter 9 when we talked about how we're taught to read word-for-word and say the words in our head as we read (subvocalization). This is a solid educational technique because children need to learn the alphabet and how to pronounce words. But after this foundation is laid, we no longer have to read in this way, because our goal isn't pronouncing words per se—it's about understanding what the words mean. Since this is the case, you can learn how to read—well, understand—groups of words (two to three) at a time.

This isn't magic or some sort of weird speed-reading technique that's without merit. In fact, you're already reading groups of words and understanding ideas behind words, signs, and abbreviations and acronyms. Think about it. When you see a common road sign, abbreviations like NYC, or acronyms like LOL or BRB, you're not reading the letters and words—you're processing the ideas behind them.

To do this, refer back to the hop method we mentioned in chapter 9. With this technique, you'll lead your eyes to see groups of words at a time and force yourself to understand the ideas behind the words versus reading them one at a time. We'll admit: this isn't something you'll learn after one or two attempts. Fight through your discouragement and plan on practicing this multiple times.

Here's one tip to consider from Tim Ferris: use a ruler to draw two equally spaced lines down the page. Then use these lines as your guide to understand groups of words. Like the hop method, you'll use these lines like rails to lead your eyes to see three to five words at a time.

Regardless of what method you use, at least practice one or the other multiple times to get a feel for it. You can't knock it until you try it.

15. Experiment with Speed-Reading Apps

For full disclosure, we have never used a speed-reading app before. But in recent years, there's been a surge in the number of these apps that promise to increase your reading speed and comprehension, and, quite frankly, they look worth giving a try.

Most of these apps use a technology called Rapid Serial Visual Presentation (RSVP). Basically, these apps will flash a single word, groups of words, or fixation points to help your eyes focus on what you're reading. Within the app, you can increase or decrease how fast the words are displayed, and in some cases you can upload text or overlay it with another app, which means you could potentially read through the news at a faster rate, for example. In every app, by flashing words in a rapid succession, the idea is that you can increase your reading speed by minimizing the time (in some cases, milliseconds) lost between words or at the end of a line on a page.

There are dozens of these apps available, and many of them have different features and benefits. If you think you could benefit from such an app, go for it. But whatever you do, don't fall for the idea that an app will help you to read and comprehend at a faster rate than what is humanly possible. Remember, we're still human, and we have some built-in limitations to how fast we can realistically read something without losing comprehension.

Over to You

There you have it: a smorgasbord of reading tips.

Don't try to absorb these all at once. Focus on those that stick out to you. Dwell on them. Commit them to heart. Take action on them. And repeat this process until you've mastered them all.

Do this, and you'll become a smarter reader—and a better leader.

Further Reading

Speaking of reading tips, here are a variety of books about reading and reading smarter:

On Reading Well: Finding the Good Life through Great Books by Karen Swallow Prior

How to Talk about Books You Haven't Read by Pierre Bayard

Why Read? by Mark Edmundson

The Reading Life: The Joy of Seeing New Worlds through Others' Eyes by C. S. Lewis

How to Read Nonfiction Like a Professor: A Smart, Irreverent Guide to Biography, History, Journalism, Blogs, and Everything in Between by Thomas C. Foster

How to Read Literature Like a Professor: A Lively and Entertaining Guide to Reading Between the Lines by Thomas C. Foster

The Pleasures of Reading in an Age of Distraction by Alan Jacobs

On the Art of Reading by Sir Arthur Quiller-Couch

How to Read and Why by Harold Bloom

Empire of Illusion: The End of Literacy and the Triumph of Spectacle by Chris Hedges

CHAPTER 14

Why You Should Join (or Start) a Book Club

A year from now you may have wished you started today.

Karen Lamb

One of the most professionally rewarding experiences of my (Jeff's) career involved not a single event, award, or milestone but rather a journey. As I entered my thirties, I landed a job unlike any I'd held before it. It was different in so many ways, including a desire among the organization's leadership to encourage my professional growth.

Prior to this experience, many of the radio stations I'd worked for didn't view the office as a place to learn new skills. You were expected to already have all the skills necessary to do the job. After all, that's why you were hired in the first place. This was especially true if you were a part of the on-air team like I was.

The energy at this station was palpable. The culture was contagious. Unlike the other operations I'd been part of, there wasn't a feeling among the staff that this place was only a stepping-stone to the next place. People wanted to work here. They enjoyed being here. And they actually liked one another.

My boss at that time, Matt, when asked about this period, said, "I think the core team we had back then all wanted to grow in leadership. We also became committed to lifelong learning. It was really an 'iron sharpening iron' experience. We made it through both good and bad times together, and we all were ready for life beyond the company based on what we learned during that season of life." What he doesn't say, but I would argue, is that the specific practices he implemented were the reasons we were committed to lifelong learning in the first place.

So how did Matt cultivate this strong desire to learn in me and those around me?

You know the answer.

It was through books, of course.

Creating Momentum through Book Clubs

Reading books as a team was not left to chance. We made a commitment. Put it on the calendar. Agreed upon a book to read. Focused on reading one book at a time. Set aside one hour each week to meet and discuss it. Through this book club, all of us were learning new skills, pushing the envelope of what was possible, and building trust among team members.

For example, in the years that followed, we were in a place of needing to work out how our organization was going to leverage social media. It was my job to figure it all out. And the leadership team put its faith in me to do just that.

So I needed to teach myself all I could about the topic. How would social media impact our industry? How could we better use it to serve our listeners? What were best practices? Which platforms made sense for our organization? These questions may seem basic today, but at that time things were rapidly changing and the pressure was on.

In those early days, I dove into books like *The New Community Rules: Marketing on the Social Web* by Tamar Weinberg and the *New York Times* bestseller *Trust Agents: Using the Web to Build Influence, Improve Reputation, and Earn Trust* by Chris Brogan and Julien Smith.

The more I read, the more untested ideas (at least in my industry) I tried. The more untested ideas I tried, the braver I became at attempting even more untested ideas. Certainly, some things worked and some didn't. But here's the real lesson I learned: in most cases, the things I tried that didn't end up going anywhere were soon forgotten. The things I tried that worked, however, began to get me noticed.

It's important to note that nothing I was doing was necessarily earth-shattering or even new, generally speaking. I was quite simply learning new skills through intentional and consistent reading, applying those new skills and ideas to my work, and making adjustments depending on the results. Anyone could have done what I did—what we did. The reality was simply that few were.

The growth I experienced and the benefits the company enjoyed all started with a book club. If not for the foresight of my boss, Matt, in starting this reading group, I would not have learned the skills I needed to succeed in my work, and the company would not have reaped the benefits of my learning.

My experience isn't an isolated case. There are several practical reasons why starting a book club can transform your team, company, or nonprofit into a powerful force.

Six Reasons Why Your Organization Should Host a Book Club

Dedicating time to book clubs is so much more than a leisure activity. Encouraging your colleagues, team, or employees to join a book club is arguably one of the most cost-effective ways you can build a healthy culture, train your team, and develop future leaders.

Let us show you why.

1. Book Clubs Foster a Healthy Work Culture

Your work culture is like a force. Not like the force you hear about in *Star Wars*. But a force that leads your organization to do what you do—or don't do. It can be a force for positive momentum or an unhealthy demotivating presence that eats away from your bottom line. Thankfully, your organization's culture isn't unchangeable; it's something you can influence for better or worse.

When influencing your work culture, keep this in mind: culture is more than your values, mission statement, and goals. It's made up of people. To influence your culture for the better, you need to positively influence your people. One often overlooked way you can do this is through a book club.

Book clubs can help you instill your company's values, build camaraderie, and boost professional development. Every benefit experienced in a book club is one way you can fuel a positive work culture. When reflecting upon his company's book club, Michael Transon, CEO of Victorious, shared a similar sentiment in an email to me (Jesse), saying, "I do believe that's an invaluable piece of organizational momentum and cultural cultivation." He added about book clubs, "They provide intentional, guarded space where the ups and downs of daily work can't distract from sharing and absorbing the principles and philosophies that guide the organization at large."

To help their growing team understand the "why" behind the decisions they make, Michael and his team at Victorious lead a book club that rereads the same book every two quarters. This way, new team members can participate and existing team members can join to dig deeper into the driving force behind the company. "The most effective decision we made was to repeatedly study the same book," said Michael. He went on to share, "It's easy to get distracted with all of the excellent content available to study. . . . If you find a truly great book, you can spend years finding the valuable nuggets and reapplying them to whatever situation your organization finds itself in."

Is there a book or a handful of books essential to your organization's culture? Don't be afraid to read them time and time again. This way you can ensure your new team members understand who you are and existing people are reminded about who you are and what you do.

2. Book Clubs Expand Team Members' Perspectives

There's one common challenge everyone faces in a book club: you don't choose every book you read. In some cases, this will be reason enough for someone to pass on joining, and sometimes for good reasons too, like personal or religious beliefs. Even though we think you should enjoy what you read, in this case, participating in a book club is valuable enough to make swallowing this bitter pill and reading whatever was picked worthwhile.

There are plenty of reasons why this is the case. First, reading outside of your preferences and comfort zone will force you to read books you wouldn't have chosen on your own. Second, when you read outside of your comfort zone, you may experience joy in discovering a new genre (or at least confirm your disdain). Third, when you're exposed to different ideas or ways of doing something, you'll discover new ways to solve whatever challenge you're facing. Finally, when reading and discussing books you wouldn't have chosen on your own, you'll be placed in a position to work through what you believe about the topic and potentially expand your viewpoint.

Don't tap out on a book club at work if you don't think you'll like the book. We challenge you to push through your initial disdain and participate—even if you only commit to the beginning to see what you think.

3. Book Clubs Lead to Growth for Everyone—Including Your Organization

Know what happens when you read books? In case you skipped chapter 2, readers improve themselves professionally and generally do better in their careers.

When you host a book club, you are paving the way for you, your peers, and your team to grow professionally. As you read books together, learn new ideas, and build better professional relationships, you'll be better able to overcome work challenges and solve problems together.

In the end, everyone benefits—including your organization.

4. Book Clubs Build an Essential Leadership Skill

Public speaking is an essential skill in leadership. We're not saying you need to be able to command the attention of thousands of people at a conference to become a leader. But developing the ability to speak clearly, confidently, and compellingly to groups both small and large will go a long way in supporting your career advancement. One way you can practice this crucial skill is in a book club.

In a book club, you will have the opportunity to publicly speak on multiple occasions. Are you providing an overview of a chapter or leading the group discussion? Treat these moments like practice for public speaking. Do you dislike impromptu discussions? Prepare your thoughts ahead of time. Is someone talking too much? Think through ways you can skillfully encourage others to participate. Does a certain member of the group tend to be argumentative? Work on ways you can defuse the situation. In time, as you practice these different situations, you'll grow more comfortable when speaking with groups.

Take this idea one notch further by picking an idea from the book you disagree with and explain why. Doing this will force you to be prepared to defend your position within a group setting and will get you used to discussing topics you have different opinions on. And you can do this when you're either leading or participating in the group.

5. Book Clubs Bolster Workplace Relationships

A book club is one surefire way you can foster community at work. At a minimum, book clubs encourage people who normally don't interact during work to meet and talk to each other. Little moments like this go a long way toward leading people to feel more comfortable with each other. Not everyone in a book club will become best friends, and that's okay. But at least you'll become more friendly, which helps everyone work better together.

Talking about working together, trust is key to workplace relationships. When you trust your colleagues, you'll be more productive, effective, and willing to work together. And trust isn't something that happens by accident. It's something that's built—or destroyed—over time.

Hosting a book club where everyone is free to share, discuss, and potentially debate ideas can create an environment that helps build trust among participants. Of course, the opposite is true if the discussion becomes heated or toxic. As you and your team grow more comfortable with each other, your confidence will naturally overflow into other situations at work too.

What is more, as you grow, learn, and adapt with others on your team, your workplace relationships will blossom along the way. In a sense, book clubs provide several essential ingredients to growing healthy relationships, including time, open communication, respect, and acceptance.

6. Book Clubs Provide a Tangible ROI

For book clubs, here's one tangible return on investment: applying the lessons you learn. As you and your book club unearth new ideas, you can apply the lessons on the job, which will make you better at what you do.

Read a book about copywriting? Experiment with new copywriting formulas in your email subject lines, social media posts, or headlines. Did you dig into a book about leadership? Reflect on your experience and identify the changes you need to make. Devour a book about marketing? Implement a new tactic you discovered.

When applying what you learn, be humble or prepared to be humbled. Reading a book is like shining a spotlight on your work. It'll give you a boost of self-confidence by revealing if you're implementing the best practices. Or it'll illuminate dark spots in your work that could make you feel like cowering in the corner. In either case, get ready to reflect on your work and make any necessary course corrections.

In some cases, applying what you learn as a group can be seamless. For example, if you host or participate in a book club with people you work with, you'll be better able to apply new ideas or tactics since everyone on your team will be on the same wavelength. In other words, everyone will know what the other person is talking about.

CHANDLER BOLT, FOUNDER OF SELF-PUBLISHING SCHOOL, ON THE READING LIFE:

The ideas that we've implemented from our internal book club are responsible for hundreds of thousands of dollars, minimum, in revenue for the company. And it just enriches the employees' lives. It makes our relationships better. We pick books like *The Five Love Languages* that really work on the whole person. So it's not just the professional side, but it's the personal side as well. It's one of their (employees') favorite things. It's a huge time to bring the company together, and it shows them how important learning is and developing them is.

Finally, after experimenting with a new lesson, make it a point to follow up afterward with the results. This will hold you and your group accountable, and you'll know whether or not it worked.

All right, now that you're (hopefully) convinced about the benefits of book clubs, it's time to start one, right? Great! Next, we'll walk you through the steps you need to take.

Seven Steps to Starting a Book Club

Starting a book club doesn't have to be complicated. To make this process as easy as possible, here are the seven steps you'll need to take.

Step 1: Get Permission (and Support)

Starting an official book club at work?

It's ideal to seek permission first—especially if you're hosting the group discussion during working hours.

When you're hitting up your boss, human resources (HR), or whomever for approval, it's also a good time to solicit their support. Ask if they are willing to purchase the books you and your group need as well as allow for the time you will need to meet. In terms of your superior's ROI, as we pointed out above, allowing you to host a book club will be a small investment of money and time compared to the big results your organization will reap in developing its team members.

Go to readtoleadbook.com/resources to download an email template you can use to obtain permission and financial support for starting a book club at work.

Step 2: Pick a Moderator

Who's leading your book discussion? Who's making the arrangements? If you're starting the book club, this will most likely fall on your shoulders or those of someone you partner with to make it happen.

As you move forward, think through whether or not you plan on leading every discussion or if you want to delegate others to have an opportunity. For what it's worth, since some of the benefits, like public speaking, are primarily experienced while leading a group discussion, we encourage you to share the love and give others the opportunity to lead too.

Step 3: Pick a Book

Picking the right book for your group is more than a shot in the dark. With millions of book choices available, and tens of thousands of books published every year, it can feel daunting to get it right, especially at first.

But rest at ease.

You'll be well on your way to narrowing down your choices after you answer these questions:

- What's your goal: professional or personal development or team building?
- Regarding development, is there a specific lesson you and your group need to learn?
- When it comes to team building, is there something timely that needs to be addressed?
- How long do you prefer the book to be?

Feel free to take the lead in choosing what book your book club will read or picking three to five options for participants to choose from. For example, I (Jesse) wanted a team I managed to go through two different books that address different gaps I perceived in our experience and skill set. The team chose what book to read first, which made it easy to know what we read next.

For the books you choose, keep them relevant to the work you do. In saying this, there is a bit of wiggle room in certain areas. In regard to relationship building, for example, my team and I read a book about the enneagram to better understand our personality types. I'll be the first to admit we haven't done the best job applying what we learned. But it was a fun exercise to read about different personality types, figure out who's who on the team, and chat about what motivates us, how we respond to stress, and more. Whatever you choose to read, be sure to make it relevant to the needs of your group.

Step 4: Set a Date and Time

Now it's time to get into the essential details: what, when, and where.

For starters, what will your book club discuss? Will you talk about the entire book in one meeting? Or do you plan on working through a few chapters at a time? To answer these questions, consider how much time everyone has to dedicate to reading the book before your meetings. This will help you think through how much reading is realistic for everyone to accomplish.

> Visit readtoleadbook.com/resources to download dozens of book suggestions to choose from. From management to self-help, we've got you covered.

Next, when will you meet? For the sake of consistency, plan on scheduling the same day and time for your book club to meet and discuss the assigned reading. In general, when you're thinking through how often to meet, if you plan on discussing an entire book, give everyone at least one month to read it. If your goal is to chat about a few chapters, then one or two weeks should do the trick.

Finally, where will your book club meet? In a conference room? Somewhere for breakfast, lunch, or coffee? Via video conference? Somewhere else? Be sure to spell out for everyone where you're going to meet.

Regardless of the choices you make, aim for your book club to be accessible, convenient, and helpful for participants.

Step 5: Read and Prepare ahead of Time

As the moderator, it's essential you're prepared ahead of time. If anyone cannot get away with not reading the book, it's you.

Before your meeting, create a list of discussion questions. To warm up your group, we recommend leading with a few easy options, such as, What did you like best or least? or, What is one thing you learned from this book? Leading with generic questions is an easy way to break the ice and get people talking.

As you prepare, pull out specific examples, points, or high-lights you made in the book for discussion. For instance, is there something crucial you want everyone to discuss or a lesson from the reading you want to highlight? Whatever it is, work it into your questions.

When thinking through your questions, consider how much time you realistically have to devote to the answers. Plan for five to seven minutes to discuss one question, and don't be surprised when follow-up questions come up and lead you down a different path. If your meeting is forty-five minutes long, then plan on preparing six to nine questions. This way you'll have more than enough material to fill the time. But again, don't be afraid to hone in on one question if the chat is helpful.

Here's one last thing to consider: you could also add your questions to an editable document (e.g., Google Docs) and share them with participants ahead of time. This will give people an opportunity to look for the answers and think about their responses. Also, if you do this, you can invite participants to add questions of their own. Before the meeting, all you'll have to do is pick the top questions you want to discuss during your time together.

Step 6: Time to Talk

It's the big day!

Your book group is meeting, and it's time to talk about the assigned reading. Sure, this can feel like a school assignment, but that doesn't mean you have to make it feel like one. For your conversation, make it easy for people to participate and strive to keep the conversation lighthearted.

In your group, there will be some who will talk too much and others you'll have to pull words out of. In both cases, get ready to handle them with grace. When someone begins to ramble, reinsert yourself into the conversation. This can be as simple as finding a way to redirect this person by

Need help coming up with questions? Go to readto leadbook.com/resources to download a list of business book club questions.

interjecting yourself, or if the situation warrants it, letting them know they're rambling and you have to move on.

When it comes to cajoling someone to talk, say something like "I'd love to hear your thoughts on this topic," or "Is there anything on your mind you'd like to share?" Afterward, give them space to participate or not. Remember, the key is to make this comfortable for everyone, which means some people may not like to talk as much.

Step 7: Implement What You Learned

Did a clear lesson or call to action emerge from your conversation? Is there something you'd like to explore further? Do you need to make any changes in your work? If anything came up during your conversation, make the time to implement what you learned. Like you would for anything else you want to accomplish, be specific, be realistic, assign the task (even to yourself), and give it a timeline.

That's all you need to know about hosting a book club. All you have to do for your following meetings is walk back through these steps. Also, feel free to adapt this process. As you lead book clubs, you'll get the hang of what does and doesn't work for you. So make it your own.

Over to You

Book clubs have been around for centuries.

From small groups meeting in pubs in England, to Christians discussing printed sermons in the 1600s, to Hannah Crocker organizing a female reading society in 1778, to General Electric encouraging employees to host book clubs in their homes in the 1940s, book clubs have been around for many years because they're good for people and organizations.

Start a book club yourself or encourage someone within your organization to take the reins. Considering the scientific benefits of reading for individuals, as well as the ways your organization can prosper, starting a book club feels like a no-brainer. These groups will help your team gel together, provide professional growth opportunities, and be good for your organization.

Further Reading

Learn more about creating a healthy business culture by reading

> *The Culture Code* by Daniel Coyle
> *Dare to Lead* by Brené Brown
> *Powerful: Building a Culture of Freedom and Responsibility* by Patty McCord

CONCLUSION

GROWING AS A READER AND LEADER

Everybody ends up somewhere in life.
A few people end up somewhere on purpose.

Andy Stanley

In the dedication of his book *Mastering the Moment*, written to a dying breed of book lovers, Tim Pollard writes that the importance of books on how our brains have developed over the centuries cannot be overstated. Through books, our once "aural brains" evolved to more "higher-level cognitive functions."[1] Books have helped to impact not just *what* we think about but also *how* we think. But for many of us, books don't hold the place in our lives they once did—if they did at all—and have been pushed out largely by digital interruptions. As a species, we're slowly being reprogrammed as to how we consume information. Shorter and faster is often perceived as "better." And the evidence suggests that our brains are again being impacted:

The brain is once again rewiring itself—only this time, in a more troubling direction. While the brains of centuries of book readers got deeper, the brains of the web generation seem to be getting shallower.[2]

Don't misunderstand us. We're not saying technology is bad. But we wholeheartedly agree with Pollard when he asserts that "everything I've learned tells me that books do still matter for the sake of the brain."[3]

With this book, Jesse and I have attempted to make the case that reading—specifically *book* reading—is the simplest and one of the most important habits you can develop, especially if your goal is to expand your influence and boost your career. We've witnessed, firsthand, the powerful impact of this habit in our own lives and careers, and in the lives and careers of every reader we know.

Our hope is that we've not only succeeded in convincing you of the impact consistent and intentional reading can have on your life and career but also equipped you with everything you need to make the most of it.

Happy reading.

Jeff Brown and Jesse Wisnewski

ACKNOWLEDGMENTS

FROM JEFF

I would like to thank:

Jesus, for strength, endurance, and the courage to say yes in the face of fear.

Annie Brown, for being a bright ray of sunshine literally every day, not only in my life but in the lives of everyone with whom you meet. My life is infinitely better for having you in it. The belief you consistently show in me means more than I could ever express. I love you!

Mom, I have you to thank for instilling in me my love of reading as a child. Thank you for all the tireless trips to the library with multiple kids in tow, and for spending time reading to us on so many occasions. You opened our eyes to a world of possibility (Prov. 22:6).

My Indianapolis family for the first thirty years (and beyond). Darin and Stacy (and their better halves, Robin and David) for being the kind of siblings to me I wish I'd been for you (and for not holding it against me). All the nieces and nephews who still call me Unka Jeef: Joey, Katelyn, DJ,

Jacob, and Rachel, you provide me a much fuller life. Uncle Dale, Aunt Bonnie, Rodney, and Brenda, some of my best memories growing up involved your family. The Clarks and the Lanes, thank you for all the laughs over the years, especially around the holidays.

All the gang at Love 98 WXIR, for being such a positive and encouraging influence on me early on; Dave, Richard, Theresa, Gary S., the late Gary A., Debbie, Nancy, Phil, Mike, Keith, and especially Louis "Chip" Gibson.

My Tennessee family, for the last twenty-five years (and beyond). Annie first and foremost, of course, but also Jean and Howard Parker. I could not ask to have been more accepted into your family. Thank you for the warm welcome. Thank you, Laura and Luke, for being among the coolest people I know. All the Powers and Street people, your clans have always been an encouragement to me.

My many friends who have supported me over the years, including the former team at 88.7 WAY-FM and their spouses: Teresa and Roger White, Tracy and Michael Cole, and the best boss in the world, Matt Austin Shuff, and his wife, Denise.

Andrea Freeman, Laura and Travis Bryant, Lynette Wright and Anne Moran, Doug and Sheryl Griffin, Bill and Janet Scott, Weston and Kerrie Brann—along with little Urban, Chappell, and Harley—Katie Jackson, Joe and Julie Leavitt and the girls, and Tammy Coonce, you are all the best of friends Annie and I could ask for.

The entire First Family family, especially Rick and Karen Blevins, Deron and Lourae Henry, Joey and Kim Scruggs, David and LeAnn Simmerman, and Steve and Kim Livengood, with a tip o' the hat to the Grissom/Brock small group.

My Power Alliance Mastermind crew: Darrell Darnell, John Dennis, and Shawn Smith. The Zone of Genius Mastermind: Brad Miller, Cassidy Cash, Drew West, Jennifer Brenton, Joe Schum, Mark Deal, Mark Hoaglin, Matt Champagne, Scott Maderer, Seth Buechley, Steve Sponseller, and Wendy Ann Gentry. You always challenged me to be better.

To Jesse, for being the best writing partner I could ask for. You are a delight to work with.

Everyone at Baker Books for being a joy to work with: Lindsey, Brian T., Brian V., Wendy, Rachel, Sarah, Olivia, Rod, Melissa, and too many others to mention.

D. J. Snell. If there is a finer literary agent in the business, I've yet to meet them.

And finally, to the authors who have inspired me the most the last twenty years: Seth Godin, Michael Hyatt, and Dan Miller, your impact on my thinking and development cannot be overstated. Liz Wiseman, Chris Brogan, Nancy Duarte, Kary Oberbrunner, and Tim Pollard, your writing continues to inspire.

FROM JESSE

Jessica, thank you for introducing me to reading, for encouraging me to be a better man, husband, and father, and for tolerating my terrible jokes. Your presence in my life is a perpetual source of inspiration.

"When will you be done with your book?" Well, Peyton, Jude, Elizabeth, Jonah, and Evelyn, it's finished. Thank you for being you and for tolerating my late nights. All of you are such a tremendous blessing, and I'm thankful to be your dad.

To my aunt Melody Holstein and the McIntyre family, especially Monty, Charlotte, Zach, Houston, and Anika. Thank you for sharing your love of reading with me.

Mickey and Betsy Neal, you are the best in-laws a guy could ask for, and thank you for your encouragement, support, and loving our family well.

Shoutout to the staff member (I'm sorry, but I've forgotten your name) at Regent University who introduced me to speed-reading in 2005. Not only did the lessons you shared with me set me up for success in graduate school, but you took my smoldering flames for reading and ignited them, which has now culminated in this book.

Thank you, D. J. Snell, for believing in us and in this project, and for being in our corner. Oh, and thank you, David and Nancy French, for making the introduction.

Thank you, Brian Thomasson, Brian Vos, and the team at Baker Books for catching the vision for this book. We're excited to encourage a new generation of readers and leaders with your support.

In closing, I want to give thanks to God. In writing this book, I was consistently reminded of your grace in my life. You have given me the ability and opportunity to express my passion for writing and to encourage and empower people to read books.

NOTES

Introduction

1. Truman Library Institute, "Truman Quotes," accessed March 6, 2021, https://www.trumanlibraryinstitute.org/truman/truman-quotes/.

Chapter 1 Why You Need to Read Like Your Career Depends on It

1. "Employee Tenure Summary," U.S. Bureau of Labor Statistics, September 22, 2020, https://www.bls.gov/news.release/tenure.nr0.htm.

2. Minda Zetlin, "9 Reasons There's Never Been a Better Time for Solopreneurs," *Inc.*, January 30, 2015, https://www.inc.com/minda-zetlin/9-reasons-there-s-never-been-a-better-time-for-solopreneurs.html.

3. Jacob Morgan, "Why Big Company Doesn't Mean Job Security," *Forbes*, November 14, 2013, www.forbes.com/sites/jacobmorgan/2013/11/14/why-big-company-doesnt-mean-job-security/.

4. "Intuit 2020 Report: Twenty Trends That Will Shape the Next Decade," *Intuit*, October 2010, http://http-download.intuit.com/http.intuit/CMO/intuit/futureofsmallbusiness/intuit_2020_report.pdf.

5. Heather Long, "The New Normal: 4 Job Changes by the Time You're 32," *CNN Business*, April 12, 2016, https://money.cnn.com/2016/04/12/news/economy/millennials-change-jobs-frequently.

6. Jaison R. Abel and Richard Deitz, "Do Big Cities Help College Graduates Find Better Jobs?" *Liberty Street Economics*, May 20, 2013, https://libertystreeteconomics.newyorkfed.org/2013/05/do-big-cities-help-college-graduates-find-better-jobs.html.

7. "Lifelong Learning is Becoming an Economic Imperative," *The Economist*, January 14, 2017, http://www.economist.com/news/special-report/21714169-technological-change-demands-stronger-and-more-continuous

-connections-between-education&sa=D&ust=1604104671289000&usg
=AOvVaw2si1vJ64WATFt9PN_78lXi.

8. "Groucho Marx Quotes," Goodreads, accessed March 6, 2021, https://www.goodreads.com/quotes/130494-learn-from-the-mistakes-of-others-you-can-never-live.

9. "Bookstores: How to Read More Books in the Golden Age of Content," YouTube video, 37:50, posted by Max Joseph, April 23, 2019, https://www.youtube.com/watch?v=lIW5jBrrsS0.

Chapter 2 Eight Research-Backed Reasons Why Readers Do Better in Their Careers

1. Michael Hyatt, "5 Ways Reading Makes You a Better Leader: The Science Behind Reading and Influence," *Michael Hyatt & Co.*, last updated January 20, 2020, https://michaelhyatt.com/science-readers-leaders.

2. University of Oxford, "Reading at 16 Linked to Better Job Prospects," *ScienceDaily*, May 9, 2011, www.sciencedaily.com/releases/2011/05/110504150539.htm.

3. University of Oxford, "Reading at 16."

4. Maja Djikic, Keith Oatley, and Mihnea Moldoveanu, "Opening the Closed Mind: The Effect of Exposure to Literature on the Need for Closure," *Creativity Research Journal* 25, no. 2 (2013): 149–54.

5. Healthline, Contributor, "Five Ways Reading Can Improve Well-Being," *Huffpost*, December 12, 2016, https://www.huffpost.com/entry/five-ways-reading-can-imp_b_12456962.

6. Greg McKeown, *Essentialism: The Disciplined Pursuit of Less* (New York: Currency, 2014), 95.

7. "Twelve Simple Tips to Improve Your Sleep," Division of Sleep Medicine at Harvard Medical School, accessed November 1, 2020, http://healthysleep.med.harvard.edu/healthy/getting/overcoming/tips.

8. Keith Oatley, "Fiction: Simulation of Social Worlds," *Trends in Cognitive Sciences* 20 (August 2016): 618–28.

9. As quoted in Shelly Levitt, "Why The Empathetic Leader is the Best Leader," *Success*, March 15, 2017, https://www.success.com/why-the-empathetic-leader-is-the-best-leader/.

10. Keith E. Stanovich, "Does Reading Make You Smarter? Literacy and the Development of Verbal Intelligence," *Advances in Child Development and Behavior* 24 (1993): 133–80.

11. IBM News Room, "IBM 2010 Global CEO Study: Creativity Selected as Most Crucial Factor for Future Success," IBM, accessed March 24, 2021, https://www.www-03.ibm.com/press/us/en/pressrelease/31670.wss.

12. Djikic, Oatley, and Moldoveanu, "Opening the Closed Mind," 149–54.

13. Cengage, "New Survey: Demand for 'Uniquely Human Skills' Increases Even as Technology and Automation Replace Some Jobs," Cengage, January 16, 2019, https://news.cengage.com/upskilling/new-survey -demand-for-uniquely-human-skills-increases-even-as-technology-and -automation-replace-some-jobs/.

14. David Grossman, "The Cost of Poor Communications," *PRovoke*, July 16, 2011, https://www.provokemedia.com/latest/article/the-cost-of -poor-communications.

Chapter 3 The Slow Death of Readers

1. David Moore, "About Half of Americans Reading a Book," Gallup News Service, June 3, 2005, https://news.gallup.com/poll/16582/about -half-americans-reading-book.aspx.

2. U.S. Bureau of Labor Statistics, "Time Spent in Leisure and Sports Activities for the Civilian Population by Selected Characteristics, Averages per Day, 2019 Annual Averages," United States Department of Labor, June 25, 2020, https://www.bls.gov/news.release/atus.t11A.htm; Christopher Ingraham, "Leisure Reading in the U.S. Is at an All-Time Low," *Washington Post*, June 29, 2018, https://www.washingtonpost.com /news/wonk/wp/2018/06/29/leisure-reading-in-the-u-s-is-at-an-all-time -low/.

3. Ingraham, "Leisure Reading in the U.S. Is at an All-Time Low."

4. Andrew Perrin, "Who Doesn't Read Books in America?," Pew Research, September 26, 2019, https://www.pewresearch.org/fact-tank/2019 /09/26/who-doesnt-read-books-in-america/.

5. Kristy Cooke, "Are People Still Reading Physical Books?" *Kantar*, March 6, 2019, https://www.kantar.com/uki/inspiration/sport-leisure /are-people-still-reading-physical-books/.

6. Perrin, "Who Doesn't Read Books in America?"

7. "What is PIAAC?," National Center for Education Statistics, accessed February 24, 2021, https://nces.ed.gov/surveys/piaac/; Melissa Block, "Casting Aside Shame and Stigma, Adults Tackle Struggles with Literacy," NPR, April 26, 2018, https://www.npr.org/sections/ed/2018/04/26/602797769 /casting-aside-shame-and-stigma-adults-tackle-struggles-with-literacy.

8. Peter Katsingris, "The Nielsen Total Audience Report," The Nielsen Report (Q1 2019), https://s3.amazonaws.com/media.mediapost.com /uploads/NielsenTotalAudienceReportQ12019.pdf#.

9. Claire Jenik, "A Minute on the Internet in 2020," *Statista*, September 21, 2020, https://www.statista.com/chart/17518/data-created-in-an -internet-minute/.

10. Amy Watkins, "Number of Commercial TV Stations in the U.S. 1950–2017," *Statista*, November 21, 2019, https://www.statista.com/sta tistics/189655/number-of-commercial-television-stations-in-the-us-since -1950/.

11. Martin Armstrong, "How Many Websites Are There?," *Statista*, October 28, 2019, https://www.statista.com/chart/19058/how-many-web sites-are-there/.

12. Robinson Meyer, "How Many Stories Do Newspapers Publish Per Day?," *Atlantic*, May 26, 2016, https://www.theatlantic.com/tech nology/archive/2016/05/how-many-stories-do-newspapers-publish-per -day/483845.

13. Read Mercer Schuchardt, *Media, Journalism, and Communication: A Student's Guide* (Wheaton: Crossway, 2018), 52.

14. NPR, "Why Doesn't America Read Anymore?," NPR, April 1, 2014, https://www.npr.org/2014/04/01/297690717/why-doesnt-america -read-anymore.

15. Tony Haile, "What You Think You Know about the Web Is Wrong," *Time*, March 9, 2014, https://time.com/12933/what-you-think-you-know -about-the-web-is-wrong/.

16. Nielsen Norman Group, "How People Read Online: The Eyetrack-ing Evidence," Nielsen Norman Group, accessed February 24, 2021, https://www.nngroup.com/reports/how-people-read-web-eyetracking -evidence/.

17. Kate Moran, "How People Read Online: New and Old Findings," Nielsen Norman Group, April 5, 2020, https://www.nngroup.com/articles /how-people-read-online/.

18. Daniel C. Richardson and Michael J. Spivey, "Part I: Eye-Tracking: Characteristics and Methods," and "Part II: Eye-Tracking: Research Areas and Application," *Encyclopedia of Biomaterials and Biomedical Engi-neering*, February 2004, http://www.eyethink.org/resources/lab_papers /Richardson2004_Eye_tracking_C.pdf.

19. Jakob Nielsen, "How Little Do Users Read?," Nielsen Norman Group, May 5, 2008, https://www.nngroup.com/articles/how-little-do -users-read/.

20. Nicholas Carr, *The Shallows: What the Internet Is Doing to Our Brains* (New York: Norton, 2011), 157.

21. Alyson Gausby, "Attention Spans," *Consumer Insights, Microsoft Canada* (Spring 2015), http://dl.motamem.org/microsoft-attention-spans -research-report.pdf.

22. Technical University of Denmark, "Abundance of Information Narrows Our Collective Attention Span," *Eurekalert*, April 15, 2019, https://www.eurekalert.org/pub_releases/2019-04/tuod-aoi041119 .php.

23. As quoted in Dream McClinton, "Global Attention Span Is Narrowing and Trends Don't Last as Long, Study Reveals," *The Guardian*, April 17, 2019, https://www.theguardian.com/society/2019/apr/16/got-a-minute-global-attention-span-is-narrowing-study-reveals.

24. Daniel Bean, "New Study Says We Pick Up Our Smartphones 1,500 Times a Week, Stare at Them 3 Hours a Day," Yahoo, October 7, 2014, https://finance.yahoo.com/news/new-study-says-we-pick-up-our-smartphones-1-500-times-a-99412542979.html.

25. "Distracted Driving," Centers for Disease Control and Prevention (CDC), October 26, 2020, https://www.cdc.gov/motorvehiclesafety/distracted_driving/index.html.

26. Gloria Mark, Daniela Gudith, and Ulrich Klocke, "The Cost of Interrupted Work: More Speed and Stress," University of California–Irvine, accessed November 1, 2020, https://www.ics.uci.edu/~gmark/chi08-mark.pdf.

Chapter 4 The Eight Biggest Reading Excuses Holding You Back

1. John Maxwell, *Leadership Promises for Every Day: A Daily Devotional* (Nashville: Nelson, 2003), 154.

2. Survey responses solicited via email, October 1, 2020; 158 responders total.

3. Berkshire Hathaway, "2013 Annual Report," https://www.berkshirehathaway.com/letters/2013ltr.pdf, 21.

4. As quoted in Stuart Murray, "The Library: An Illustrated History," Internet Archive, accessed March 10, 2021, https://archive.org/details/libraryillustrat0000murr/page/80/mode/2up.

5. Francis Bacon, "Of Studies," accessed March 6, 2021, https://www.psy.gla.ac.uk/~steve/best/BaconJohnson.pdf.

6. As quoted in Herbert Lui, "Read 50 Pages Before Deciding to Drop a Book," Lifehacker, November 19, 2014, https://lifehacker.com/read-50-pages-before-deciding-to-drop-a-book-1660458546.

7. "Automobile University—Zig Ziglar," YouTube video, 1:50, posted by Ziglar Inc. January 5, 2012, https://www.youtube.com/watch?v=S1XZOXMXmAA

8. David B. Daniel and William Douglas Woody, "They Hear but Do Not Listen: Retention for Podcasted Material in a Classroom Context," *Sage Journals*, June 29, 2010, https://journals.sagepub.com/doi/abs/10.1080/00986283.2010.488542.

9. Morton Ann Gernsbacher, Kathleen R. Varner, and Mark Faust, "Investigating Differences in General Comprehension Skill," *Research Gate*, June 1990, https://www.researchgate.net/publication/21016436_Investigating_Differences_in_General_Comprehension_Skill.

10. Gausby, "Attention Spans."

Chapter 5 Six Ways to Know What You Should (and Shouldn't) Read

1. As quoted in Harriet Rubin, "C.E.O. Libraries Reveal Keys to Success," *New York Times*, July 21, 2007, https://www.nytimes.com/2007/07/21/business/21libraries.html.

2. As quoted in Harriet Rubin, "What CEO's Book Collections Say about Them," *New York Times*, July 20, 2007, https://www.nytimes.com/2007/07/20/business/worldbusiness/20iht-libraries.4.6757114.html.

3. Tom Jacobs, "Home Libraries Provide Huge Educational Advantage," *Pacific Standard*, June 14, 2017, https://psmag.com/education/home-libraries-provide-huge-educational-advantage-14212.

4. Michiko Kakutani, "Transcript: President Obama on What Books Mean to Him," *New York Times*, June 16, 2017, https://www.nytimes.com/2017/01/16/books/transcript-president-obama-on-what-books-mean-to-him.html.

5. The idea for this question, and a few others in this chapter, was inspired by a worksheet by Ryan Holiday called "Build Your Anti-Library." Learn more about his "Read to Lead: A Daily Stoic Reading Challenge" at https://dailystoic.com/read.

Chapter 6 Too Busy Not to Read

1. Marc Brysbaert, "How Many Words Do We Read per Minute? A Review and Meta-Analysis of Reading Rate," Department of Experimental Psychology, Ghent University, April 12, 2019, https://psyarxiv.com/xynwg/.

2. Shea Bennett, "This Is How Much Time We Spend on Social Networks Every Day," *Adweek*, November 18, 2014, http://www.adweek.com/digital/social-media-minutes-day/.

3. David Cohen, "How Much Time Will the Average Person Spend on Social Media During Their Life? (Infographic)," *Adweek*, March 22, 2017, http://www.adweek.com/digital/mediakix-time-spent-social-media-infographic/.

4. John Koblin, "How Much Do We Love TV? Let Us Count the Ways," *New York Times*, June 30, 2016, https://www.nytimes.com/2016/07/01/business/media/nielsen-survey-media-viewing.html?mcubz=1.

5. Seth Fiegerman, "Time Wasters: 11 Mind-Blowing Stats," *The Street*, December 4, 2009, https://www.thestreet.com/slideshow/12810753/1/time-wasters-11-mind-blowing-stats.html.

6. Jory MacKay, "Screen Time Stats 2019: Here's How Much You Use Your Phone during the Workday," *Rescue Time*, March 21, 2019, https://blog.rescuetime.com/screen-time-stats-2018/.

7. Garland Vance, *Gettin' (un)Busy: 5 Steps to Kill Busyness and Live with Purpose, Productivity, and Peace* (Author Academy Elite, 2019).

8. Sarah Berger, "These Are the States with the Longest and Shortest Commutes—How Does Yours Stack Up?," *CNBC Make It*, February 23, 2018, https://www.cnbc.com/2018/02/22/study-states-with-the-longest -and-shortest-commutes.html.

Chapter 8 How to Absorb a Book into Your Bloodstream

1. Mortimer J. Adler and Charles Van Doren, *How to Read a Book: The Classic Guide to Intelligent Reading* (New York: Touchstone, 1972), 49.

2. The idea for this chapter and several points pertaining to writing in books are inspired by Demian Farnworth, "How to Absorb a Book Into Your Bloodstream," *Copybot*, accessed March 4, 2021, https://thecopybot .com/absorb-book-bloodstream/.

3. Olga Khazan, "How to Learn New Things as an Adult," *Atlantic*, March 16, 2017, https://www.theatlantic.com/science/archive/2017/03 /how-to-learn-new-things-as-an-adult/519687/.

4. Adler and Van Doren, *How to Read a Book*, 193.

Chapter 9 Double (or Triple) Your Reading Speed in Minutes

1. Soumyaranjan Nayak, "Role of Music in Helping You Focus," *Toppr*, January 3, 2017, https://www.toppr.com/bytes/music-help-focus/.

2. Mark Seidenberg, "Sorry, But Speed Reading Won't Help You Read More," *Wired*, January 24, 2017, https://www.wired.com/2017/01/make -resolution-read-speed-reading-wont-help/.

Chapter 10 How to "Read" a 220-Page Book in One Hour

1. H. Y. McClusky, "An Experiment on the Influence of Preliminary Skimming on Reading," *Journal of Educational Psychology* 25 no. 7 (1934): 521–29, https://psycnet.apa.org/record/1935-00842-001.

2. G. B. Duggan and Stephen J. Paine, "Text Skimming: The Process and Effectiveness of Foraging through Text under Time Pressure," *Journal of Experimental Psychology: Applied* 15, no. 3 (September 2009): 228–42, https://researchportal.bath.ac.uk/en/publications/text-skimming -the-process-and-effectiveness-of-foraging-through-t.

3. Keith Raynert et al., "So Much to Read, So Little Time: How Do We Read, and Can Speed Reading Help?" *Psychological Science in the Public Interest* 17 (January 2016): 4–34.

4. Thanks to Demian Farnworth for his insight into this reading technique.

Chapter 11 How to Create an Unchangeable Reading Habit

1. Daniel H. Pink, "The Power of Habits—And the Power to Change Them," *Daniel H. Pink*, accessed March 8, 2021, https://www.danpink.com/2012/03/the-power-of-habits-and-the-power-to-change-them/.

2. "Will Durant Quotes," Goodreads, accessed March 6, 2021, https://www.goodreads.com/quotes/546495-we-are-what-we-repeatedly-do-excellence-therefore-is-not.

3. James Clear, *Atomic Habits: An Easy & Proven Way to Build Good Habits & Break Bad Ones* (New York: Avery, 2018), chapter 3.

4. "How Long Does It Take for a New Behavior to Become Automatic?" *Healthline*, accessed March 6, 2021, https://www.healthline.com/health/how-long-does-it-take-to-form-a-habit.

5. Jack F. Hollis et al., "Weight Loss during the Intensive Intervention Phase of the Weight-Loss Maintenance Trial," *American Journal of Preventative Medicine* 35, no. 2 (August 2008): 118–26, https://pubmed.ncbi.nlm.nih.gov/18617080/.

6. Benjamin Harkin et al., "Does Monitoring Goal Progress Promote Goal Attainment? A Meta-Analysis of the Experimental Evidence," *Psychological Bulletin* 142, no. 2 (February 2016): 198–229; https://pubmed.ncbi.nlm.nih.gov/26479070/.

7. Jeff Brown, "The Future of Behavior Design with Dr. BJ Fogg," *Read to Lead with Jeff Brown*, podcast, June 23, 2020, https://readtoleadpodcast.com/324-the-future-of-behavior-design-with-dr-bj-fogg-and-jeff-brown-of-read-to-lead-podcast/.

8. Gabrielle M. Turner-McGrievy and Deborah F. Tate, "Weight Loss Social Support in 140 Characters or Less: Use of an Online Social Network in a Remotely Delivered Weight Loss Intervention," *Translational Behavioral Medicine* 3 (2013): 287–94.

9. Maxwell, *Leadership Promises for Every Day*, 234.

Chapter 12 The Key to (Nearly) Mastering Anything

1. "Most Powerful Speech: The 3 Rules to a Less Complicated Life," YouTube video, 6:27, posted by Goalcast on October 30, 2017, https://www.youtube.com/watch?v=8YFTJuJkrts.

2. John B. Horrigan, "Lifelong Learning and Technology," Pew Research Center, March 22, 2016, https://www.pewresearch.org/internet/2016/03/22/lifelong-learning-and-technology/.

3. Andrew Perrin, "Who Doesn't Read Books in America?" Pew Research Center, September 26, 2019, https://www.pewresearch.org/fact-tank/2019/09/26/who-doesnt-read-books-in-america/.

4. Andrew Perrin, "One-in-Five Americans Now Listen to Audiobooks," Pew Research Center, September 25, 2019, https://www.pewresearch

.org/fact-tank/2019/09/25/one-in-five-americans-now-listen-to-audio
books/.

5. Peep Laja, Twitter post, January 13, 2020, 11:31 a.m., https://twitter
.com/peeplaja/status/1216774897587888128.

6. Jeff Haden, "These 10 Scientific Ways to Learn Anything Faster
Could Change Everything You Know about Dramatically Improving
Your Memory," *Inc.*, December 13, 2018, https://www.inc.com/jeff-haden
/these-10-scientific-ways-to-learn-anything-faster-could-change-every
thing-you-know-about-dramatically-improving-your-memory.html.

7. Josh Kaufman, *The First 20 Hours: How to Learn Anything . . .
Fast!* (New York: Portfolio, 2014).

8. Johns Hopkins, "Want to Learn a New Skill? Faster? Change Up
Your Practice Sessions," Johns Hopkins Medicine, January 28, 2016,
https://www.hopkinsmedicine.org/news/media/releases/want_to_learn
_a_new_skill_faster_change_up_your_practice_sessions.

9. Art Markman, "Test Yourself to Learn Better," *Psychology Today*,
August 23, 2011, https://www.psychologytoday.com/us/blog/ulterior-
motives/201108/test-yourself-learn-better.

10. Aubrey Francisco, "Ask the Cognitive Scientist: Distributed Practice," *Digital Promise: Accelerating Innovation in Education*, May 8,
2019, https://digitalpromise.org/2019/05/08/ask-the-cognitive-scientist
-distributed-practice/.

11. Colin M. MacLeod et al., "The Production Effect: Delineation
of the Phenomenon," *Journal of Experimental Psychology: Learning,
Memory, and Cognition* 36, no. 3 (May 2010): 671–85, https://pubmed
.ncbi.nlm.nih.gov/20438265/.

Chapter 13 Fifteen Tips on How to Read Smarter

1. J. Edward Glancy, "An Encouragement to Read (or Reread) John
Bunyan's *The Pilgrim's Progress*," *Knowing & Doing*, February 26, 2018,
https://www.cslewisinstitute.org/An_Encouragement_to_Read_John
_Bunyans_The_Pilgrims_Progress_FullArticle.

2. Catherine Clifford, "Billionaire Warren Buffett Discusses the Book
that Changed His Life," *CNBC Make It*, February 2, 2017, https://www
.cnbc.com/2017/02/02/billionaire-warren-buffett-discusses-the-book-that
-changed-his-life.html.

3. As quoted in Ryan Holiday, "Books to Base Your Life On (The Reading List)," *Ryan Holiday*, accessed November 1, 2020, https://ryanholiday
.net/reading-list/.

4. As quoted in Maria Popova, "Umberto Eco's Antilibrary: Why
Unread Books Are More Valuable to Our Lives than Read Ones," *Brain*

Pickings, March 24, 2015, https://www.brainpickings.org/2015/03/24
/umberto-eco-antilibrary/.

5. Kevin Hendricks, "Reading Habits Questions," September 25, 2020, personal email.

Conclusion

1. Tim Pollard, *Mastering the Moment: Perfecting the Skills and Processes of Exceptional Presentation Delivery* (Washington, DC: Conder House Press, 2019), dedication page.

2. Pollard, *Mastering the Moment.*

3. Pollard, *Mastering the Moment.*

ABOUT THE AUTHORS

JEFF BROWN is an award-winning radio producer and personality and a former nationally syndicated morning show host. After more than twenty-five years in the radio and music industries, Jeff went boss-free and launched the *Read to Lead* podcast, a four-time Best Business Podcast nominee. Jeff has interviewed hundreds of authors, all leaders in their respective industries, including Seth Godin, Simon Sinek, John Maxwell, Liz Wiseman, Dr. Henry Cloud, Brian Tracy, Nancy Duarte, Stephen M. R. Covey, and Alan Alda. He lives in Tennessee with his wife, Annie, and their three dachshunds.

JESSE WISNEWSKI is a senior-level marketing professional and a self-proclaimed bibliophile. He has been featured in *Forbes*, *CNBC Make It*, *The Muse*, *Observer*, and more. He holds a master's degree from Gordon-Conwell Theological Seminary and a marketing degree from Marshall University.

Ready to
ACCELERATE
YOUR READING?

Get free access to each of the resources referenced in this book, including:

- Time tracking and scheduling tools
- A reading plan spreadsheet
- Dozens of conversation-starter questions for books clubs
- And more

Start learning faster today at
readtoleadbook.com/resources.

To inquire about speaking at your event, organizing virtual and in-person training for your team, or leading personal and professional growth-driven workshops for your organization, please write to **contact@readtoleadbook.com**.

Get connected to
JEFF BROWN

🐦 @THEjeffbrown

💼 @brownjeff

📘 @thejeffbrown

📷 @thejeffbrown

Get connected to
JESSE WISNEWSKI

🐦 @thejessew

💼 @JesseWisnewski

📘 @Jesse.wisnewski

Listen to the
READ TO LEAD PODCAST

If you love reading, then you'll love this podcast. If you desire to stretch and grow by reading more but haven't been able to make it happen, then you'll find encouragement here. And in the meantime, you'll learn more than you ever thought possible. *Read to Lead* is a four-time Best Business Podcast nominee.

Available wherever you get your podcasts.